FAMILY USA

FAMILY USA

FRANK BARRETT

B XTREE

First published in Great Britain in 1993 by Boxtree Limited

Text © copyright Frank Barrett 1993

10 9 8 7 6 5 4 3 2 1

Printed in Finland, by WSOY

Boxtree Limited
Broadwall House
21 Broadwall
London SE1 9PL

A CIP catalogue entry for this book is available from the British Library

ISBN 1 85283 522 2

Cover design by Robert Updegraff

Front cover photograph courtesy of Tony Stone Images

CONTENTS

FOREWORD

For a growing number of British travellers, America has become the one and only holiday destination. Chat to holiday-makers in departure lounges at Gatwick, Heathrow or Manchester, and you will hear from many people who will tell you that the States is now the only place they will consider taking a holiday. Talk to property agents in Orlando, Florida (a number of whom are British) and they will report booming sales to a British clientele. Despite the regular reports of muggings and other violent attacks on foreign tourists in America (particularly Florida), the numbers of British visitors to the States goes on increasing year after year.

Indeed America is in many ways the perfect destination for a family holiday. But the perfect American holiday needs careful planning. To get the best out of the trip you need to know exactly what is available - and equally you should be sure what sort of holiday you and your family want.

This book will provide most of the answers to your questions. It sets out the various alternatives: it compares holiday places in America; lists the specialist companies; offers a battle plan for coping with Orlando; even provides recommendations for a weekend in New York.

In writing this book I am indebted to the United States Travel and Tourism Administration which supplied prompt answers to my questions. I am grateful to over 100 tour operators who took the trouble to offer a detailed reply to my questionnaire. I have to say that most of the hard work in producing this book was done by Sheila Barrett, without whose help it would all have been impossible.

To anybody planning to travel to America for a holiday, I wish you an excellent trip.

Frank Barrett
December 1993.

INTRODUCTION

THE AMERICAN DREAM

When I was a child in South Wales our house lay under the flight path followed by aircraft flying across the Atlantic. I can remember many sunny summer days lying on my back in the grass looking up at the planes high overhead scurrying westwards. I often lay watching until the long, white vapour trail left by each aircraft began to disappear, and I would wish hard that one day I too might be on a plane flying to America.

Any child of the sixties who was a regular visitor to the cinema, watched television or read comic books, had travelled in his head to America a hundred times a week. But in those days actually going there for real was an impossible dream – I might just well have wished to fly to the moon. Transatlantic air travel was a rich man's privilege. Transatlantic liners had always had cheaper berths in the less agreeable parts of the ship, but generally these were taken by people emigrating or travelling to join friends and relatives.

Leisure travel to America was a pleasure enjoyed only by a wealthy elite. When in the sixties jet-powered planes like the Comet, the Boeing 707 and the DC-8 finally rendered the liners obsolete and suddenly expanded the possibilities offered by air travel, those wealthy enough to fly the world inevitably became known as the jet set. In the Sixties, the prospect of 'ordinary' people ever being able to fly to America would have seemed faintly absurd. Even the less expensive charter flights then being operated in increasing numbers to the Mediterranean were still beyond most people's means.

Cheaper air travel to America eventually became possible in the seventies for two reasons. Firstly, the development of the Boeing 747 'jumbo' jet and its imitators, the Lockheed Tristar and the McDonnell Douglas DC-10, allowed airlines to carry passengers long distances much more cheaply than the previous generation of jets. The other reason was a man called Freddie Laker. His long legal battle in the seventies to launch his Skytrain service to New York transformed the transatlantic airline business.

Laker Airways began life as a package-holiday charter airline,

1

but by the early seventies it was heavily involved in cheap charter flights to North America. Under absurd rules devised by the airline cartel IATA (the International Air Transport Association) to make cheap air travel hard to get, charter passengers to the States had to be members of an 'affinity' group: six months' membership of the group was a condition of travel.

The rules were openly flouted. Organizations like the Midland Dahlia society and the Birmingham Rose Growers Association developed a membership which seemed more interested in getting low-cost transatlantic travel than in matters horticultural. Membership cards and tickets for those seeking a cheap flight with an 'affinity group' were easily available at the airports.

After falling foul of the authorities who enforced the bizarre IATA affinity requirements, in 1971 Laker proposed a simpler system: an air service that operated more like a train. People would simply turn up at the airport without booking and take off at a cheap fare. Laker proposed to call the service Skytrain. Attempting to offer airline passengers value for money doesn't seem particularly extraordinary now, but in the seventies the concept was practically revolutionary. Until the coming of Skytrain, the world's airline business had been run to suit the airlines rather than the needs of the consumer.

The launching of the Laker Skytrain service to New York in 1977 – and subsequent services to Los Angeles and Miami – triggered a revolution in air travel. Laker's competitors, the major national carriers, argued that offering cheaper fares would not mean carrying more people – they believed they would carry the same amount of travellers, but for less total revenue.

They couldn't have been more wrong. Laker's new cheap fares – and the cheaper fares that his rivals were forced to offer in order to compete – attracted a massive new market of people who had always wanted to visit America but who had hitherto never been able to afford it.

The statistics tell their own story. In 1960, for example, just 94,000 British people visited America; 10 years later this had risen to just under 300,000 people, reaching 533,000 in 1977. In 1978, the first full year of Laker Skytrain, the number of travellers to America shot up by an astonishing 42 per cent to 757,000 – and increased again the following year by 32 per cent to 930,000. Laker's effect on the transatlantic market was astonishing. In 1982, the year he was forced into bankruptcy, a total of 1.2m British people flew the Atlantic. With Laker's departure the transatlantic market declined, slumping to 861,000 in 1985.

But by now a second Laker had arrived on the aviation scene: Richard Branson and his Virgin Atlantic airline. Benefiting from Laker's experience, Branson ushered in a new competitive era launching services to New York, Miami, Boston, Orlando and Los Angeles.

Numbers of people travelling to the US boomed once more: in 1986 it was up to 1.1m – and by 1990 had dramatically leapt ahead of the Laker years to reach an astonishing 2.5m. In 1992 the total was 2.8m and in 1993 it is expected to break the 3m mark. While other holiday destinations have had their ups and downs, since 1985 travel to the US has increased every single year.

The latest figures show that America is the fourth most popular overseas holiday destination for the British with a 7 per cent share of the market: first is France (24%); second Spain (16%) and third, the Irish Republic (7.5%). Of the long-haul destinations (i.e. excluding Europe, the Mediterranean countries and North Africa), the US is the clear favourite with 46%, followed by Canada (7%); the Caribbean (7%); Australia and New Zealand (6%) and the Middle East (4%).

A DREAM COME TRUE

It was thanks to the Laker-inspired price war that in 1978 I was finally able to afford to make my first trip to the States. At the grand old age of 24 I flew with my wife on TWA to New York. I was fully prepared to be disappointed: after all, my expectations were so great, it seemed impossible that they could have been matched by the reality.

But I was not disappointed: that first trip to the America remains etched in my memory in every wonderful detail. I can remember aching for that first glimpse of the Manhattan skyline on the drive into the city from the airport, thinking it would never come – and then suddenly there it was, the most thrilling sight in the world. I feasted on that fantastic jumble of skyscrapers and tower blocks amazed that I could instantly identify the Empire State Building, the Chrysler Building and the twin towers of the World Trade Centre. To see that New York actually existed as one had always imagined it was almost as stunning as finding out that Father Christmas was alive and well and living in Greenland.

It is embarrassing now to recall how overawed we were. For the first day we were almost too frightened to put a foot outside our elegant Central Park hotel: stepping into the buzz and pace of the sidewalks from the security of the hotel lobby seemed as wise as setting sail on the stormy waters of the Atlantic on a li-lo.

But after a short period of acclimatization where we clung together in a state bordering on animal terror, we gradually gave ourselves up to the Big Apple. Muggers were not waiting on every corner. In this expectation alone we were confounded. New York in every other particular was every bit as we imagined. Taxi drivers were abusive, sirens wailed non-stop, steam poured from man hole covers, people told you to 'have a nice day', coffee shop waitresses asked you if you wanted your breakfast eggs fried 'over easy'. That wish made long ago in South Wales to fly to the States had at last come true.

I have returned every year to America and that initial excitement has never waned. Shortly after that first trip to New York, I travelled to Los Angeles (as a passenger on the inaugural Skytrain service) and this visit opened up a fresh box of delights: here was the city of Hollywood, Sunset Boulevard, Beverly Hills, the Universal Studios tour, Disneyland and the surf of a dozen Beach Boys records.

Subsequent trips took me to Florida, Chicago, Kansas City, San Francisco, Washington DC, Alaska – each new part of America offered that same delicious thrill. The pleasure, for example, of waking early to watch breakfast television (there is no better way of getting an insight into daily American life); tucking into the traditional American breakfast – perfect for a vegetarian like me – with hash browns or French toast with maple syrup; driving on big American roads in a car with power steering, automatic transmission, cruise control and air-conditioning; cheap, well-appointed hotels and motels; efficiently run and good value restaurants and fast-food places; shops that sell Levi jeans for less than £15 per pair; cinemas that show films six months before they appear in Britain.

For me the supreme attraction of America, as it has been for generations of emigrants and travellers, is that it is a Big Country of infinite travel possibilities. Drive eastwards for 24 hours from the English Channel and you would be nudging the western fringes of the Middle East. Drive westwards for 24 hours from New York and you would barely have reached Chicago. Such a big country with such a diverse racial mix means that it can satisfy a multitude of different sorts of holiday-makers. It is however, above all, a place for family holidays.

When my son was just nine months old we had no hesitation in taking him to New York. He survived a storm-tossed crossing on the QE2 rather better than we did. Toting him around the streets of Manhattan in a push-chair was no more difficult than Bath.

But our real family holidays to America began five years later when we took our first trip to Disney World in Florida. My son was five and my daughter was three and we all found the experience overwhelming. The second week we spent in the relative peace of Sanibel Island on the Gulf Coast of Florida. Florida may seem like a very long way to go for a traditional beach holiday, but it would be hard to beat the shell-strewn beach of Sanibel Island. We played on the beach, splashed in the pool and studied alligators and eagles in the island's nature reserve.

Three years later we returned for a second encounter with Disney in Orlando, and this time it was a stunning success. We devoured the Magic Kingdom, EPCOT, the Disney-MGM Studios – and, above all, the superb Disney-run Typhoon Lagoon water slide park. The second week of this American holiday was spent driving down the Mississippi from St Louis to New Orleans and we almost had just as good a time as we had in Florida. The children loved the absurd Presley mansion of Graceland, enjoyed staying as bed and breakfast guests at a Plantation house and were enthusiastic about the relaxed style of New Orleans.

Even without any Disney sights to see or theme parks to experience, the children are happy enjoying the simple things of America: the fast-food, for example, or the endless children's TV. And they love visiting America for the reasons that I was desperate to visit America as a child: America is the place that they see often in films, on television and in books. America continues to be exciting to visitors of all ages.

WHO CHOOSES AMERICA?

America being the sort of marketing-driven country it is, you would not be surprised to learn that the United States Travel and Tourist Administration has carefully analysed the 'key demographics' of visiting travellers.

Of the British arrivals in 1991, for example, the average male age was 40.8 years, average female age 38.2 years; average annual family income was £45,000. Nearly one-third travelled on organized packages, with nearly 15 per cent choosing a fly/drive package. The average British traveller took 74 days to decide on his destination and booked the trip 50 days in advance.

Top activities on an American holiday were: shopping (80%); dining in restaurants (79%); sightseeing in cities (59%); watersports/sunbathing (49%); touring countryside (43%); visiting amusement/theme parks (39%).

The top states visited were: Florida (37%); California (27%); New York (23%); Massachusetts (8%); Texas (7%). The top cities visited were: Orlando (27%); New York City (21%); Disney World (15%); Los Angeles (14%); San Francisco (14%).

But when potential travellers were asked which states they were most interested in travelling to, the answers were: California (65%); Florida (48%); New York (38%); Arizona (19%); Texas (10%); Louisiana (9%); Nevada (8%); Washington DC (7%); Washington state (7%).

WHY CHOOSE AMERICA?

The main reason why people choose a holiday in America can be explained in one word: Florida – or if you wanted two words with a conjunction: Disney and Florida. Orlando has now taken its place among the likes of Palma, Malaga and Alicante as one of the principle package holiday airports.

Well over a third of the 2.8m British people who visited America in 1992 took their holiday in Florida. It is in many ways the perfect holiday place: a good year-round climate (though some would say too hot and humid in the summer – but not too hot and humid for the British!), dozens of theme parks and animal parks, cheap accommodation and excellent value food and drink.

In the past five years, charter flights to Orlando have become a staple of the package holiday business. It is not necessarily a cheap holiday, but by any standards it is always excellent value. With return flights to Orlando from £200, car hire from £80 per week, and a three-bedroom house with swimming pool, dishwasher and air-conditioning available from £400 per week – added to the cost of admission to Disney World and other theme parks – a family of four is unlikely to have much change from £2500 for a two-week trip.

In Florida, however, you can be sure of having the time of your life. You would have to be a redoubtable cynic not to enjoy at least some part of Disney World (which includes EPCOT, Disney-MGM studios and the magnificent Typhoon Lagoon). There is also Universal Studios, the Kennedy Space Centre, Busch Gardens – even a Tupperware Museum! (Not to mention dozens of 'factory outlet' shops where you can buy Reeboks for £20 and Levi jeans from £10 a pair.)

And there's much more to Florida than simply Orlando and Disney. Miami is just a four-hour drive away: have a look at the Art Deco district of Miami Beach. There are the Florida Keys. And the Gulf Coast of Florida has several superb resorts – Sanibel and Captiva Island, for example, are delightful havens of peace and quiet with an enthralling nature reserve.

Florida may often be crass, loud, larger than life and occasionally dangerous – but it is always good fun. There is nowhere in America like Florida, there is nowhere in the world like Florida. You meet people who will now never go anywhere except Florida for their annual holiday. Orlando, for example, has thousands of holiday homes owned by British people.

But just as there is more to Florida than Disney World and Orlando (Florida's Keys and the Everglades, for example, would be star holiday attractions anywhere in the world) – there is much, much more to America than Florida. You could have a perfectly splendid time having American vacations which never once ventured beyond the confines of the Florida state line, but you would be missing out on a superb country which offers tens of thousands of different sorts of holiday places and a million varieties of holiday.

After Florida, the next major attraction for British visitors on the east coast is, of course, New York. Broadway shows, peerless art galleries and museums, fine shops – and a tireless energy – help make New York an unforgettable experience. It can also be a surprisingly inexpensive short break: by judiciously shopping around it is possible to organize a three-night stay for around £350 – including return air travel.

Three nights in New York is probably sufficient. The pleasure of America is picking up a hire car and heading for the highway. North-east of New York lies Boston and the exquisite countryside of New England, particularly magnificent during the Fall when the autumn colours of the leaves are a delight. But almost anywhere in the States offers good touring country. Head to St Louis, for example, and follow the Mississippi south to New Orleans – driving through Memphis (home of the Presley mansion Graceland). En route you can stay at *antebellum* mansions which these days make their living not from cotton or slaves but bed and breakfast (see below).

The ultimate destination for the free-wheeling traveller is California. Cruising the highway with the top down and a Beach Boys song playing on the radio is a dream that can come true. There's much more to California than Los Angeles, Hollywood and Disneyland (but if there was only LA, it would be enough!).

To the north of LA, San Francisco is a day's drive: en route you can visit fascinating sights such as the Hearst castle at San Simeon. North of San Francisco is the wine country of the Napa Valley. South of LA lies San Diego and the Mexican border. From LA you are also a day's drive from Las Vegas which provides a base for exploring the Grand Canyon.

Do you want an activity holiday? You could try cycling in New England, hiking in the Blue Mountains of Virginia, boating on the Great Lakes, white water rafting down the Colorado river, horse-riding in Utah, skiing in Aspen – or what about mountain biking in Marin County near San Francisco where mountain biking and the mountain bike were first invented?

If you want a less strenuous break, you could confine yourself to brisk city centre walks: New York, Boston, Washington DC, New Orleans, Chicago, San Francisco – each one has enough shops, museums, art galleries and other attractions to provide sufficient amusement to keep any reasonably curious traveller occupied for a fortnight.

But America is above all a country that begs to be explored by rail, by Greyhound bus, by plane or by hired car. Accommodation is generally very cheap: motels and the cheaper hotel chains offer outstandingly good value. To cut costs further, an increasing number of accommodation places offer self-catering facilities: one- or two-bedroom suites with fully equipped kitchens at the same price you would pay for a medium-priced hotel room. America's well-stocked supermarkets provide memorably inexpensive excursions for the self-catering traveller.

MAKING A CHOICE

The choice of holidays and holiday destinations in America seems infinite. Even if you just want to go to Disney World in Florida you will face the task of choosing between the competing arrangements of over 100 operators. And you will have to decide how long you want in Orlando – and should you spend a week somewhere else? More than any other destination, a successful holiday in America requires careful planning. Choose rashly and you could not only waste several hundred pounds on unnecessarily expensive travel arrangements – you might choose quite the wrong destination.

Over the next couple of hundred pages, you should find all the information necessary to choose the sort of American holiday that will be right for you.

THE BEST OF AMERICA

This a brief list of my favourite holiday things in America – I would be pleased to hear your nominations (the best recommendations will earn a free edition of the revised *Family USA*).

The Cheapness of it All

Throughout most of 1993, the Pound chugged along at about $1.40, a far cry from the heady days of 1980 when a pound bought $2.40 and the British invasion of Florida began in earnest. But while the rate now may be low, things are much better than they seem. Over the past 10 years wage levels and the cost of living have risen faster in Britain than in the US, the result is that it has never been cheaper to take a holiday in America.

With petrol costing from around 65p a gallon, a Big Mac on offer for 40p, a decent motel room available for around £20 and US supermarket prices in dollars what we pay in pounds (this means that many things are about half the price they are in Britain) – an American holiday is the ultimate travel bargain. The question is not whether you can afford to go this summer – but whether you can afford not to go.

Best Airline

The best British airline on the transatlantic is without doubt the tirelessly innovative Virgin Atlantic (0293 562000); I don't think any of the American transatlantic airlines are particularly outstanding – the one I like best is probably American Airlines (071-834 5151).

See chapter 2

Best Hotel Chain

America is the land of the good value hotel and motel: finding a cheap place is often just a matter of cruising and checking the boards outside each property to see who is offering the best deal. Expect to pay from around £20 for a reasonable motel.

My favourite of all the chains is Marriott (0800 221222/071-439 0281): like most of the big chains it offers a hotel 'product' to accommodate different sectors of the market – from five-star hotels for business men to self-catering 'residences' for families. I can honestly say that of all the different sorts of Marriott I have stayed in, I have yet to find a Marriott I didn't like. All I can hope is that heaven will be like a Marriott hotel.

See chapter 5

Bed and Breakfast

This is one of the best ways of meeting real Americans – and enjoying good inexpensive accommodation. Fodor's and Frommer's both publish guides to bed and breakfast accommodation in the States, normally rooms in private houses but furnished to a surprisingly high standard. Expect to pay around £50 bed and breakfast for a good house and a warm welcome.

See chapter 5

Best American Sight

The best sight in the most literal sense is a toss-up between that first glimpse of the Manhattan skyline and the wonderful spectacle of San Francisco's Golden Gate Bridge. I also get a thrill from seeing the 'Hollywood' sign on the hill above Tinsel Town.

See chapters 7 and 9

Best Theme Park

No contest here: Disney World is more than just a place of amusement, it's a huge, great work of art. I think it's impossible to get tired of its various attractions. Most favourite bits include: Thunder Mountain, Pirates of the Caribbean, Space Mountain and the Haunted Mansion; in Disney-MGM I love The Great Movie Ride.

See chapter 8

Best American Experience

For the real American experience, you need to stay in an American home: shopping at American supermarkets will make you realise what you have been missing all these years at Sainsbury's or Waitrose. You can house swap or you can rent. Since property prices are cheap in the States, so are rental costs. Big self-catering properties – houses with up to four bedrooms with private pools in Orlando, for example, cost from under £500 per week.

See chapter 4

Best Specialist Operator
Bon Voyage (0703 330332) is a leading US specialist full of information on all aspects of travel to the States from air passes and bus travel to coach tours.

See chapter 10

Best Guidebook
The Rough Guide to the USA (Penguin, £12.99) is the most concise and certainly the best written guide to the whole country. One to read before you go and also one to have with you on your trips.

I hope you enjoy *Family USA*: if you have any comments, suggestions or recommendations, please write to me at PO Box 67, Bath.

1

PLANNING A HOLIDAY

Do you want to take an independent trip? Or would you prefer to buy an inclusive package? While America is the perfect place for the independent traveller, if you are planning a holiday in Florida or California – or a short break to a city like New York or Los Angeles, then buying a package makes good sense.

Being independent provides you with total freedom: you fly with the airline you want, from the airport you select, to the destination that you choose at the times which suit you. If you want to tour around, an independently-organized trip is probably the only sensible choice. (An increasing number of specialist tour operators (see chapter 6) will be happy to put together such a trip entirely to your specifications, if you would prefer to trust this task to an expert.)

If you are planning your first trip to the States, the advantage of buying a package is that you have an operator to hold your hand at every step of the way. There will probably be somebody at your departure airport to sort out any problems; you will be met in America by a representative; and while you are in the States, there will be somebody available from the holiday company to offer help and advice (even if this just amounts to an answer-phone on which you can leave messages).

The choice between package or independent really depends on what suits you. There will be probably very little difference in price. Even though tour operators have the benefit of the economies of scale resulting from bulk purchase of airline seats and hotel rooms, you can probably put together your own American package for little more – and perhaps – for a little less than a tour operator.

Remember that for most months of the year, America is a buyer's market for the traveller. There are normally far more aircraft seats on offer than there are passengers to fill them. Flights, particularly charter flights to Florida, are often heavily discounted – sometimes these discounts are not just late-booking deals.

Similarly with car hire and hotel rooms in the States, there are usually deals to be had for the asking. The recession has hit the American tourist industry hard: bad news for them, good news for you. Remember therefore to shop around, compare prices – and never be afraid to ask for a discount. Americans expect to be asked for a special deal: if you don't ask, you won't get.

FINDING OUT INFORMATION

Many people choose a holiday destination on a whim – picking a hotel or a resort simply because it looks nice. Nobody in their right mind would spend money on a car simply because they liked the look of it on the garage forecourt, yet this is often the glib way that many people select a holiday. The secret to a successful holiday is good planning and the making of the right, informed choices. You may, for example, have decided that you want to go to Florida. Yet Florida offers a multitude of holiday choices – by careful planning you can organize your vacation time to see the selected sights as comfortably as possibly.

There are several sources of information. The American government and the individual states produce useful maps and guides (see below for further information).

The USTTA (United States Travel & Tourism Administration) office in London used to be open to the public – but no longer. The USTTA (PO Box 1EN, London W1A 1EN) now only deals with written requests for its information pack (send a postcard with your name and address on it and allow a week for delivery): alternatively you can request the information pack by fax by telephoning 071-439 4377. The USTTA telephone number 071-495 4466 offers a recorded message telling callers where to get information about Greyhound buses, Amtrak and US visas.

Apart from guidebooks (see below), perhaps the best source of tourist information about the US are the individual states, each of which has its own tourist office which can offer a wide range of valuable publications.

US State Tourist Offices

Alabama
Bureau of Tourism & Travel,
532 South Ferry Street,
Montgomery AL 36014
Tel: (205) 242-4169

Alaska
Division of Tourism,
Deptartment of Commerce & Economic Development,
PO Box E,
Juneau AK 99811
Tel: (907) 465-2015

Arizona
Office of Tourism,
1100 West Washington Street,
Phoenix AZ 85007
Tel: (602) 542-8687

Arkansas
Deptartment of Parks &
Tourism,
One Capitol Mall,
Little Rock AR 72201
Tel: (501) 682-7777

California
Office of Tourism,
1121 L Street,
Suite 103,
Sacramento CA 95814
Tel: (916) 322-1396

Colorado
Tourism Board,
PO Box 38700,
Department CVB,
Denver CO 80238
Tel: (303) 592-5510

Connecticut
State Information Bureau,
165 Capital Avenue,
Hartford CT 06106
Tel: (203) 842-2200

Delaware
State Tourism Service,
PO Box 1401,
99 Kings Highway,
Dover DE 19903
Tel: (302) 736-4271

Florida
Division of Tourism,
126 Van Buren Street,
Tallahassee FL 32301
Tel: (904) 487-1462

Florida Tourism UK Office,
Florida House International,
18/24 Westbourne Grove,
London W2 5RH
Tel: 071-727 1661

Georgia
Department of Industry &
Trade,
285 Peachtree Center Avenue
NE,
Suite 1000,
Marquis Two Tower,
Atlanta GA 30303-1232
Tel: (404) 651-9038

Hawaii
Hawaii Visitors Bureau,
Waikiki Business Plaza,
2270 Kalakaua Avenue,
Honolulu HI 96815
Tel: (808) 923-1811

Idaho
Idaho Travel Council,
700 West State Street,
Room 108,
State Capitol Building,
Boise ID 83720
Tel: (208) 334-2470

Illinois
Illinois Office of Tourism,
620 East Adams Street,
Springfield IL 62701
Tel: (217) 782-7500

Indiana
Indiana Division of Tourism,
One North Capitol,
Suite 700,
Indianapolis IN 46204
Tel: (317) 232-8860

Iowa
Iowa Division of Tourism,
200 East Grand Avenue,
Des Moines IA 50309
Tel: (515) 242-4705

Kansas
Kansas Travel & Tourism
Division,
400 SW 8th Street,
Topeka KS 66603-3450
Tel: (913) 296-2009

Kentucky
Office of Tourism
Development,
2200 Capital Plaza Tower,
500 Mero Street,
Frankfort KY 40601
Tel: (502) 564-4930

Louisiana
Office of Tourism,
PO Box 94291,
Capitol Station,
Baton Rouge LA 70804-9291
Tel: (504) 342-8142

Maine
Publicity Bureau,
97 Winthrop Street,
Hallowell ME 04347
Tel: (207) 289-2423

Maryland
Department of Economic &
Community Development,
Office of Tourist Development,
217 East Redwood Street,
Baltimore MD 21202
Tel: (301) 333-6611

Massachusetts
Department of Commerce &
Development,
Division of Tourism,
100 Cambridge Street,
Boston MA 02202
Tel: (617) 727-3201

Michigan
Travel Bureau,
PO Box 30226,
Lansing MI 48909
Tel: (517) 373 0670

Minnesota
Travel Information Center,
250 Skyway Level,
375 Jackson Street,
St Paul MN 55101
Tel: (612) 297-2901

Mississippi
Department of Economic
Development,
PO Box 849,
Jackson MS 39205
Tel: (601) 359-3927

Missouri
Division of Tourism,
PO Box 1055,
Jefferson City MO 65102
Tel: (341) 751 4133

Montana
Department of Commerce,
Montana Promotion Division,
1424 9th Avenue,
Helena MT 59620-0401
Tel: (406) 444-2564

Nebraska
Department of Economic
Development,
Division of Travel & Tourism,
PO Box 94666,
Lincoln NE 68509
Tel: (402) 471-3796

Nevada
Department of Economic
Development,
Travel and Tourism Division,
515 South Carson Street,
Carson City NV 89710
Tel: (702) 687-4322

New Hampshire
Office of Vacation Travel,
PO Box 856,
105 Loudon Road,
Concord NH 03301
Tel: (603) 271-2666

New Jersey
Department of Commerce &
Economic Development,
Division of Travel & Tourism,
20 West State Street,
Trenton NJ 08625-0826
Tel: (609) 292-2470

New Mexico
Economic Development &
Tourism Department,
1100 St Francis Drive,
Santa Fe NM 87503
Tel: (505) 827-0318

New York City
New York City CVB,
Two Columbus Circle,
New York NY 10019
Tel: (212) 397-8222

New York State
Division of Tourism,
1 Commerce Plaza,
Albany NY 12445
Tel: (518) 474-4116

North Carolina
North Carolina Travel and
Tourism Division,
430 North Salisbury Street,
Raleigh NC 27611
Tel: (919) 733-4171

North Dakota
Tourism Promotion Division,
Liberty Memorial Building,
600 East Boulevard,
Bismarck ND 58501
Tel: (701) 224-2525

Oklahoma
Tourism & Recreation
Department,
500 Will Rogers Building,
Oklahoma City OK 73105
Tel: (405) 521-3981

Oregon
Economic Development
Department,
Tourism Division,
775 Summer Street NE,
Salem OR 97310
Tel: (503) 378-3451

Pennsylvania
Bureau of Travel Development,
Department of Commerce,
416 Forum Building,
Harrisburg PA 17120
Tel: (717) 787-3453

Rhode Island
Department of Economic
Development,
Tourism and Promotion
Division,
Gilbane Building,
7 Jackson Walkway,
Providence RI 02903
Tel: (401) 277-2601

South Carolina
Division of Tourism,
1205 Pendleton Street 522,
Columbia SC 29201
Tel: (803) 734-0129

South Dakota
Department of Economic &
Tourism Development,
711 Wells Avenue,
Pierre SD 57501
Tel: (605) 773-3301

Tennessee
Department of Tourist
Development,
PO Box 23170,
Nashville TN 37202
Tel: (615) 741-2158

Texas
Tourism Division,
PO Box 12008,
Austin TX 78711
Tel: (512) 463-8585

Utah
Utah Travel Council,
Council Hall,
Capitol Hill,
Salt Lake City UT 84114
Tel: (801) 538-1030

Vermont
Travel Division,
Agency of Development &
Community Affairs,
134 State Street,
Montpelier VT 05602
Tel: (802) 828-3236

Virginia
Virginia State Travel Service,
1021 East Cary Street, 14th
Floor,
Richmond VA 23219
Tel: (804) 786-4484

Washington
Department of Commerce &
Economic Development,
Travel Development Division
101 General Administration
Building,
Olympia WA 98504-0613
Tel: (206) 586-3024

**Washington District of
Columbia**
Department of Tourism,
Washington Convention &
Visitors Association,
1575 I Street,
NW Washington DC 20005
Tel: (202) 789-7000

West Virginia
Travel West Virginia,
State Capitol Complex,
2101 Washington Street,
East Charleston WV 25305
Tel: (304) 348-2286

Wisconsin
Department of Development,
Division of Tourism,
PO Box 7970,
Madison WI 53707
Tel: (608) 266-7621

Wyoming
Wyoming Division of Tourism,
I-25 at College Drive,
Cheyenne WY 82002
Tel: (307) 777-7777

Guidebooks

The other major source of useful information and advice on America are guidebooks. Probably second only to France, America has a huge choice of travel guides which cover every possible aspect of the country. Visit a good bookshop and spend some time browsing in the travel section and you will discover a number of guides which will provide invaluable information and useful advice.

Useful books and maps to look out for include:

The Rough Guides are good, practical, thoughtful books. *USA: The Rough Guide* (Rough Guides, £12.99) and *California and West Coast USA: The Rough Guide* (Rough Guides, £9.99) are highly recommended. Also worth looking at for an overall view of holidays and travel in America is *Let's Go USA* (Pan, £14.99).

For local regional and city guides, the Frommer's series is worth a look. The *Frommer's New Orleans City Guide 93-94* (Prentice Hall, £8.99), for example, is a useful companion. The Access series is also well put together. For example, *Boston Access* (Harper Collins, £9.99) tells you all you need to know about the city. The Smithsonian guide series is excellent for history, museums and culture – the books are handsomely produced with fine colour illustrations: for example, *The Smithsonian Guide to Historic America: The Deep South* (Stewart, Tabori & Chang, £10.95) is good reading to plan your trip, invaluable to have with you as you travel around and, on your return home, provides a marvellous souvenir of your holiday.

There are plenty of New York guides on the market. *The Time Out New York Guide* (Penguin, £9.99) is good value. The newest New York guide *Eyewitness Travel Guides: New York* (Dorling Kindersley, £14.99) is a superb book chock full of information and invaluable advice.

For Disney World, there is really only one guide worth buying: *The Unofficial Guide to Walt Disney World 1993* (Prentice Hall, £8.99) by Bob Sehlinger.

Other Americans publications I like include: *Budget Dining & Lodging in New England* (Globe Pequot Press, £7.95); *Journey to the High Southwest: A Travellers' Guide* (Globe Pequot Press, £13.95) by Robert Casey.

Specialist travel bookshops in the UK include:

Daunt Books for Travellers, 83 Marylebone High Street, London W1 (071-224 2295): Fascinating shop owned and managed by James Daunt where books are arranged geographically.

Stanfords, 12-14 Long Acre, London WC2E 9LP (071-836 1321): Stanfords has been serving the needs of the independent traveller since 1851; the management claims that Stanford's 16 staff is ready to offer expert advice on the shop's stock of 20,000 maps and books. Stanford's can also handle inquiries by phone or mail.

Travel Bookshop, 13 Blenheim Crescent, London W11 2EE (071-229 5260): New and second-hand books with over 12,000 titles covering guidebooks as well as background works on art, history and wildlife – and also fiction. Mail order service: send s.a.e. for special lists. Credit card orders taken on telephone.

Travellers' Bookshop, 25 Cecil Court, London WC2N 4EZ (071-836 9132): The shop also has a good selection of new and second-hand travel books.

Waterstones, 121–125 Charing Cross Road, London WC2 (071-434 4291): The Charing Cross branch has the best range of travel books, but the other 13 shops in London and the 87 elsewhere in the UK have a comprehensive range.

PASSPORTS

To enter the US you will need a full British passport (not the 12-month Visitors' passport available from Post Offices). This is valid for 10 years and is available from the Passport Offices listed below: an application form is available from main post offices. A 32-page passport costs £15; a 48-page passport costs £22.50.

Passport Offices

Liverpool
Passport Office,
5th Floor,
India Buildings,
Water Street,
Liverpool L2 0QZ
051-237 3010

London
Passport Office,
Clive House,
70 Petty France,
London SW1H 9HD
071-279 3434

Newport
Passport Office,
Olympia House,
Upper Dock Street,
Newport,
Gwent NPT 1XA
0633 244500/244292

Peterborough
Passport Office,
Aragon Court,
Northminster Road,
Peterborough PE1 1QG
0733 895555

Scotland
Passport Office,
3 Northgate,
96 Milton Street,
Cowcaddens,
Glasgow G4 0BT
041-332 0271

Northern Ireland
Passport Office,
Hampton House,
47–53 High Street,
Belfast BT1 2QS
0232 232371

VISAS

America may be the Land of the Free, but it is a country not quite free of its affection for red tape. British citizens are no longer required to have a visa, but the situation is not as clear cut as it may seem.

If you wish to stay in America for less than 90 days, you can avoid having to get a visa by filling out the Visa Waiver Form which you will normally get from the airline, either when you check-in or else on the plane. This form must be completed and handed to immigration officials on arrival in America. If you are planning to stay in the US for longer than 90 days you will need a non-immigrant visa available from the US Embassy in London (071-499 7010) or from the US Consulates in Edinburgh (031-556 8315) or Belfast (0232 228239).

On the flight to the States you will be given an Immigration Form which you will have to complete and present with your passport at the Immigration Desk.

Passing through Immigration in America is an incredibly protracted business. You will almost certainly have to queue (if the wait is less than 15 minutes, you can count yourself lucky). Each person's details are checked on computer which informs the Immigration Office whether you are an undesirable alien or whether you have outstanding traffic fines from a previous visit (which you have to pay before you are admitted into the country!). If you are of student age or look as if you might be coming to America to seek employment (or both), you will be closely questioned on what you intend to do in America. Show that you can support yourself financially and make it absolutely clear that you have absolutely no intention to take up employment.

Fortunately, after a recent change in procedure to follow the European example of a red and green channel, customs examination has been greatly speeded up. Customs people are anxious to know whether you have fresh food on you (you shouldn't have) or whether you have recently been on a farm (they fear you may be importing some terrible disease that may kill off the entire cattle population of the Mid West).

If you are 17 the duty-free allowance is 200 cigarettes and 100 cigars; visitors over 21 are allowed to bring in a litre of spirits or wine. This provides an early warning that in America the legal age of buying alcohol from bars or liquor stores is 21 – a rule that tends to be very rigidly enforced. Even if you are well over 21 don't be surprised to be asked for an ID. On her 30th birthday, my wife was delighted to be asked for proof of her age in an LA restaurant before they would serve her with a beer.

You should also bear in mind that returning from America to Britain, your allowance for goods bought in America is only £36 – a limit that is rigidly enforced. Customs officers will sometimes even check your wallet for receipts and credit card vouchers to see whether you have exceeded the limit.

DRIVING LICENCE
You will need to show your UK driving licence before you can hire a car (so will other members of the party if they wish to share the driving). An International Driver's Permit is not necessary.

HEALTH AND INSURANCE
There is no need for any vaccinations or other medical precautions. The only medical precaution necessary is a financial one. Most British people are nowadays aware of the perils of falling ill in the States. There have been widespread reports of heart attack victims who, on being discharged, have been presented with bills

of £250,000 (an event likely to precipitate a second attack!). When you realise that in America standard medical bills amount to an average cost of £3000 per day, it becomes clear why you need to be properly insured. (Many hospitals will probably not let you across their thresholds unless it is clear you will be able to pay their bills.)

You need to have insurance which will not only be sufficient to cover you against medical costs in excess of £1m (most of the best policies will ensure that you are flown home to Britain). The policy will also offer cover against other routine hazards such as cancellation and theft.

ELECTRICITY

Unlike Europe where they have different plugs but the same sort of electricity, in America they not only have different plugs they also have different electricity: 110V AC. While hairdryers and electric shavers may be switched to the different voltage, other electrical equipment will probably need a transformer.

TAKING MONEY

A credit card is practically indispensable. Hotels and car hire companies, for example, may refuse to let you have a room or rent you a car without sight of a credit card. Not having a credit card suggests that you are either an undischarged bankrupt or an escaped criminal. If you want to rent a car and organize accommodation without a credit card, you will need to make prior arrangements (you will have to pay in advance, for example).

A credit card will cover most of your purchases, from buying gas (petrol) to your hotel bill. With you PIN number you can also use your credit card to get money out of automatic cash dispensers (since these machines occasionally swallow cards for no obvious reason, it may be wise not to travel with one credit card as your sole source of funds).

For incidental expenses, the safest way to take money is in dollar traveller's cheques (sterling traveller's cheques will be greeted with incredulity in America). Dollar traveller's cheques are used like cash in shops and restaurants.

Have sufficient dollars in cash with you when you arrive at least to meet your immediate requirements: tips for porters, telephone calls, taxi fares or road tolls.

SAFE TRAVELLING IN AMERICA

Over the past 12 months there seems to have been constant stream of news reports of British and other foreign tourists in America who have been attacked, shot or killed during violent robberies.

Florida

This is the main danger area for tourists – particularly Miami – since tourists can easily stray accidentally into areas of high crime. (And criminals are near at hand to prey on careless tourists.)

If you are arriving in Miami, do not pick up your car after dark: stay at a nearby hotel overnight. Before leaving the car-hire depot, make sure you have full directions and a map showing how to reach your destination. Do not leave the main highway unless you are sure you know where you are going.

If you are lost, go to some other exit; or go back to your point of origin; or look for an identifiable police vehicle. If you break down, pull over, raise the bonnet, lock yourselves inside and wait for a police vehicle to stop. If someone bumps your vehicle from behind – or yells that your car is disabled and signals that you should stop, do not believe them. Drive to a safe place where there are a lot of people before getting out of your car. Always keep the doors to your car locked and your windows rolled up.

Never leave anything visible in your car or anything valuable in it, visible or not, when you park it. If you see someone with a car that looks as if it has broken down, beware: it may be a trap. Drive to a public telephone and call the emergency number: 911.

When driving from Miami airport, do not get off at any of the following exits: if you are on I-95 (Interstate highway 95) avoid NW 119th, 103rd, 95th, 79th, 69th, 62nd, 8th or 2nd streets; if you are on the SR 112 (State Road 112) expressway, which links Miami airport with the Julia Tuttle Causeway/I-195 to Miami Beach, avoid all exits on the Miami side, except those for the airport and for Biscayne Boulevard (US 1). If you are on the SR 836 (State road 836) expressway, which links Miami airport with the MacArthur Causeway/I-395 to Miami Beach, avoid the exits for NW 12th Avenue and for Biscayne Boulevard/NE 2nd Avenue); if you exit at NW 27th Avenue, use only the south-bound exit.

In Orlando, the biggest risk comes from muggers: if threatened, hand over everything that is demanded. Do not resist: if you argue you increase the chances of being shot.

Washington DC

In big cities like New York, Washington DC and New Orleans bear in mind that safe areas sit immediately alongside dangerous areas – sometimes separated by no more than a city block. Risky areas will be dangerous even by daylight. In New York, for example, do not venture by foot or public transport beyond southern Manhattan up to Harlem or the Bronx. If in doubt: avoid public transport, do not walk – take a taxi.

The bare statistics for Washington DC seem terrifying. If

Greater London had the same murder rate as Washington DC, 15 Londoners would be variously shot, knifed or beaten to death every day. Fortunately, as always, statistics are misleading. True, the American capital does suffer from 450 murders, or more, every year, but the vast majority of them occur in parts of the city that tourists never wittingly intend to visit. Also the vast majority of murders are within families, or among drug pushers and rival gangs.

With very few exceptions, downtown and the sightseers' paradise of monumental Washington are perfectly safe, as are Georgetown and the affluent white neighbourhoods of north-west DC. Steer clear, however, of any foray into the north-east or south-east, especially at night. Parts of north-west Washington east of 14th Street are also best avoided. There are also other pockets of potential trouble: around the Capitol by night, the drug- and prostitute-infested streets around Logan Circle where a British tourist was shot dead during 1993, and occasionally the Mount Pleasant district two miles north of the White House, where rioting occurred two years ago.

New York
In Manhattan, some of the safest places are now some of the more dangerous and vice versa, but there are still no maps declaring the mugging and drug zones. Tourists usually find a hotel in mid-town – between 40th and 60th streets and between Madison and Sixth Avenue. That's where most of the hotels are, and the on- and off-Broadway theatres. The area is bounded by 42nd Street to the south and Central Park to the north. In the good old days, when the Broadway strip stretched further south and was bursting with energy and pride, 42nd Street was a fine place to be. Then it was taken over by strip shows and erotic movie theatres, and then those closed, leaving a filthy, smelly, largely abandoned street. Now, from the point that 42nd crosses Seventh Avenue and on westward, across 8th, 9th and 10th Streets to the Hudson River, the area is considered dangerous, even by the local cabbies. Keep to active theatreland.

On the other hand, Greenwich Village, which has always been a place to buy drugs and thus had more than its share of muggings, has been cleaned up quite a bit. The square and the surrounding tiny streets of the old French Quarter are safe to walk around during the day, and relatively so at night. Also, Union Square, six blocks to the north, used to be a dope peddlers' paradise, but now has a farmer's market four times a week, excellent restaurants and children's playgrounds.

Unless you have business, or a special point of interest such as a museum, keep out of Harlem, which means staying south of

125th Street or thereabouts. Anywhere north, east or west of Columbia University at 116th and Broadway can put you at risk, even in daylight. Go to the zoo, but not beyond it in the Bronx.

Keep out of any park at night, and in the daytime in Central Park stick to the areas where there is a lot of activity, such as the zoo, the boating pond and the carousel. When in doubt take a taxi rather than the subway, and if you venture underground wear your 'subway look' – permanently moody and prone to dinosaur-type ferocity.

New Orleans
Adrian Strasser, an Edinburgh schoolteacher, was murdered in April 1993 in the inner-city fringes around the popular French Quarter. As the French Quarter is somewhere tourists are likely to visit, it is very advisable to call at the New Orleans Visitor Information Center, where staff will indicate on maps those areas and streets they think tourists should avoid.

Los Angeles
It is called the City of Angels, but much of it might equally be Where Angels Fear to Tread. Most visitors tend to avoid the city's southern and eastern areas, a huge tract of urban landscape otherwise known as gangland. The risks tend to be exaggerated, although you only need to watch the local television news, with its wall-to-wall murders, rapes and robberies, to understand why people are cautious. Many Angelenos do not venture south of the Santa Monica freeway (the '10' that dissects the city east-west to the Pacific Ocean), regarding it as a no-go area. If you do go exploring, do so with great care.

An epidemic of car-jackings has heightened public nervousness, but it should be stressed that they only affect a tiny percentage of motorists in the metropolis. If you are an unlucky victim, hand over the keys without resisting. Car thieves are often armed.

The tourist areas in the region – Disneyland, Universal Studios, Venice Beach, Santa Monica and Malibu – are considered safe during the day. It is wise to exercise extra vigilance in Hollywood, the squalid area around the Walk of Fame and Mann's Chinese Theatre, which has a high crime rate and tends to be a gathering point for petty thieves and drug addicts. As in any city, you are strongly advised to lock your car at all times, avoid parking in unlit areas and keep a sharp eye on personal belongings.

2

GETTING TO AMERICA

There is really only one way of getting to America: by plane. The Cunard Line continues to operate regular sailings of the *QE2* from Southampton to New York, but while this is a perfectly pleasant way of travelling (if you have five days to spare for the crossing), most people will want to fly.

Most air services are inevitably concentrated on the major centres of American population such as New York, Chicago and Los Angeles (or the main holiday destinations such as Miami and Orlando), but there are now direct flights to a wide range of US destinations from a surprisingly large number of UK airports.

Direct scheduled flights

From	*To*	*Airline*
London		
Gatwick	Atlanta	Delta Air Lines
Gatwick	Baltimore	US Air
Gatwick	Boston	Northwest Airlines
Gatwick	Boston	Virgin Altantic
Heathrow	Boston	American Airlines
Heathrow	Boston	British Airways
Gatwick	Charlotte	US Air
Heathrow	Chicago	American Airlines
Heathrow	Chicago	British Airways
Heathrow	Chicago	United Airlines
Gatwick	Cincinnati	Delta Air Lines
Gatwick	Dallas/Fort Worth	American Airlines
Gatwick	Dallas/Fort Worth	British Airways
Gatwick	Denver	Continental
Gatwick	Detroit	Delta Air Lines
Heathrow	Detroit	British Airways
Gatwick	Honolulu	Continental
Gatwick	Houston	British Airways
Gatwick	Houston	Continental
Heathrow	Los Angeles	Air New Zealand

From	To	Airline
Heathrow	Los Angeles	American Airlines
Heathrow	Los Angeles	British Airways
Heathrow	Los Angeles	United Airlines
Heathrow	Los Angeles	Virgin Atlantic
Gatwick	Miami	Delta Air Lines
Gatwick	Miami	Virgin Atlantic
Heathrow	Miami	American Airlines
Heathrow	Miami	British Airways
Gatwick	Minneapolis	Northwest Airlines
Gatwick	New York	British Airways
Gatwick	New York (Newark)	Continental
Heathrow	New York	Air India
Heathrow	New York	American Airlines
Heathrow	New York	British Airways
Heathrow	New York	El Al
Heathrow	New York	Kuwait Airlines
Heathrow	New York	United Airlines
Heathrow	New York	Virgin Atlantic
Heathrow	New York (Newark)	Virgin Atlantic
Gatwick	Orlando	Virgin Atlantic
Heathrow	Orlando	British Airways
Heathrow	Orlando	Delta Air Lines
Heathrow	Philadelphia	British Airways
Heathrow	San Francisco	British Airways
Heathrow	San Francisco	United Airlines
Heathrow	Seattle	British Airways
Heathrow	Seattle	United Airlines
Heathrow	Washington	British Airways
Heathrow	Washington	United Airlines

Birmingham

Birmingham	New York	British Airways

Manchester

Manchester	Atlanta	Delta Air Lines
Manchester	Chicago	American Airlines
Manchester	New York	American Airlines
Manchester	New York	British Airways

Glasgow

Glasgow	Boston	Northwest Airlines
Glasgow	Chicago	American Airlines
Glasgow	New York	British Airways

Airline telephone numbers
Air India (071-491 7979)
American Airlines (0800 010151)
British Airways (0345 222111)
Continental (0293 776464)
Delta Air Lines (0800 414 767)
El Al (071-437 9255)
Kuwait Airlines (071-412 0007)
Northwest Airlines (0345 747800)
TWA (071-439 0707)
United (0800 888 555)
US Air (0800 777 333)
Virgin Atlantic (0345 747747)

GETTING A CHEAP AIR FARE

Until about 20 years ago, transatlantic air travel was a closely regulated business. Scheduled airlines had two levels of fare: first (extremely expensive) and economy (very expensive). The introduction of charter flights provided a new cheap alternative.

Laker's Skytrain produced the major breakthrough, for the first time forcing the major scheduled airlines to offer competitive rates. While the competition has been wholly beneficial for the consumer, it has also inevitably caused some confusion. If you ask a travel agent who has the cheapest fare to New York, you will discover that a one word answer is out of the question. It all depends on what sort of ticket you want, when you intend to travel and how long you plan to stay in America.

Over the past 15 years, transatlantic airlines have suffered the problem of too many seats and not enough passengers to fill them. Today, for example, there are more than 20 scheduled flights from Heathrow and Gatwick to New York – a total load of around 10,000 seats to be filled to just one US destination on one single day. The airlines will be happy if they fill two-thirds of their aircraft. The result of this over-capacity is that on a pence per mile basis air fares to America remain among the cheapest in the world.

Anxiety about poor bookings frequently persuades the `Big Three': American Airlines, British Airways and United Airlines to embark on a new round of price cutting in order to stimulate bookings. Fares vary according to season, and according to supply and demand. Outside the peak period you can expect to get to New York for as little as £179 return, and to Los Angeles from just £240 – but at peak periods these prices will more than double. Leading low-fare specialists worth contacting first include STA Travel (071-937 9971) and Trailfinders (071-937 5400).

Some of the best deals are for flights on indirect routes: via

Dublin, Amsterdam, Finland or even Reykjavik in Iceland. These deals are often available with free connecting flights from your local UK airport so they are well worth considering. The best transatlantic buys are likely to be found to Florida: huge over-capacity on charter flights to Orlando is still providing huge price cuts – check around the small ads for return seat-only deals from £179.

Most of the major tour operators run seat-only programmes which allow you to book charter deals up to six months in advance. Prices for these seats are reasonable for out-of-season departures but expensive for high season: you might consider it's worth paying extra to be sure of getting away on the day you want. Throughout the year, however, there is a thriving business in discounted charter tickets; as the departure date for a flight approaches, operators slash prices in order to make a sale. There are several sources for charter deals including: Avro (0293 567916); Cosmos (061-480 5799); Meridian Tours (071-493 4312); Owners Abroad 061-745 7000); Unijet (0444 458181); Vivair (071-636 5466).

Courier flights

The fast growing international courier business is always on the look-out for people who will fly as a courier in return for a cut-price air fare. Little effort is involved – someone checks you in at the departure airport, and someone is there to meet you on arrival to handle the paper work. The fares can be very cheap: for example, £179 return for a trip to New York.

Courier Travel Services (071-351 0300) and Polo Express (081-759 5383) are the two companies to contact for further information. Expect to join a long waiting list.

Round-the-world tickets

In the late seventies, the now defunct US airline Pan Am introduced a startling new concept in air travel: the round-the-world air fare. In those halcyon pre-deregulation days, Pan Am was run more as an arm of the American foreign office than a commercial airline, and it did actually run an air service that went right round the world.

The round-the-world service was later scrapped, but the low-cost round-the-world fare remained. It was an idea that was rapidly taken up by rival airlines, who began to band together in groups of two and three in order to come up with fares that spanned the globe.

Ever since Jules Verne's Phileas Fogg went round the world in eighty days, the idea of circling the earth has held a particular fascination. It is, after all, the ultimate trip. So far it has proved particularly popular with the under-26s, especially with those who have recently graduated and who are keen to see the world before entering full-time employment. If you are planning a trip to the West Coast of the States, for example, for only a little more expenditure you could upgrade your flight to a round-the-world trip.

The one problem about the fares is that there are so many options available, and each is extraordinarily complex. In theory, most travel agents should be able to offer advice; in practice they can be of little genuine assistance.

Round the world travel does not cost as much as you might think. The official fares – those published by the airlines themselves and on sale through appointed travel agencies start from under £1000. You can choose from fares offered by a combination of more than forty airlines on some 200 routes connecting nearly 500 cities – nearly all of which include America. With most carriers the number of stop-overs you may make is unlimited within the validity of your ticket which usually lasts from six to twelve months.

A round-the-world fare which allows the journey London to Delhi, Bangkok, Sydney, Auckland, Los Angeles, New York to London is being offered by STA Travel (071-937 1733) for £759. The ticket is valid for 12 months.

Agencies that offer special round-the-world deals:
Airline Ticket Network (0800 727747); Austravel (071-734 7755); Bridge the World Travel Centre (071-911 0900); Columbus Travel (071-929 4251); STA Travel (071-937 9962); Trailfinders (071-938 3366).

BY SEA
The liner *QE2* owned by Cunard (071-491 3930) offers the only regular sea crossing from Britain to America. It offers attractive package deals. For example, the *QE2* Super Value Holiday packages include a five-day transatlantic crossing on the *QE2*, two or three nights' accommodation in New York and a transatlantic flight, with prices starting at £595.

3

GETTING AROUND IN AMERICA

In Britain we consider the business of getting from London to Manchester or from Birmingham to Plymouth as rather a substantial journey. In America, such a trip of a couple of hundred miles would be dismissed as nothing more than a short hop. Distances are, of course, relative. In a country as big as America, in the time it takes to fly from Los Angeles to New York, you could fly from New York to London.

For the commercial development of America, a system of fast efficient communications was vital. From the railways through the automobile to the Jumbo Jet, America has always had the best – and the best value – in travel. The railway system may not be what it was during its heyday (but to their credit the Americans are now investing heavily in trains and other mass transit systems), but there is no doubt that in road and air travel the Americans are incredibly well served.

For the traveller on a budget and with time to spare, the Greyhound bus offers a superb way to see America. But for people who want to see as much of America as possible in a brief stay, airlines offer the best way of getting around. It is a small American town indeed that has no airport and no link to the region's major airport which will offer connections north, east, south and west.

And since airlines were deregulated at the end of the seventies, fares are now usually keenly priced. Competition is never less than fierce: when bookings slump, airlines respond immediately with a spate of special offers. The airlines also offer attractive air passes which allow travellers to skip across the country as if they were hopping around London on a Red Bus Rover ticket.

For drivers, the American roads also offer an easy passage from state to state. Wide freeways with regular service stations and restaurants offer rapid journeys (even though you are limited by law to speeds of no more than 55mph or 65mph).

Whether you are travelling by plane, bus, train or car, America really is the country of the Easy Rider...

AIR TRAVEL

US Air Passes

American airline air passes are one of the benefits of US deregulation which took place 10 years ago. Faced with a sudden need to fill seats at whatever price they could get for them, airlines came up with the air pass: unlimited travel for a fixed period of days. Its immense popularity forced most airlines to modify the concept, providing coupons to be used for each flight rather than allowing unlimited season ticket travel. Even so, the air passes still offer extraordinarily good value.

The best of the current deals include:

Delta Air Lines Stand-by Pass:

Unlimited stand-by pass in continental USA. Cost $499 (£332) for 30 days or $799 (£532) for 60 days. Available if used in conjunction with either transatlantic or transpacific flights or both.

Northwest Airlines Stand-by Pass:

Thirty days stand-by pass on mainland North America including Canada, for $499 (£332). Available if used in conjunction with return transatlantic flight.

TWA Air Pass:

    Three coupons: £183
    Four coupons: £244
    Five coupons: £305
    Additional coupons: £23 (maximum 10 coupons permitted)
One coupon = one flight; two free transits are allowed on each coupon at St Louis, New York and Atlanta. The air pass is only available to passengers flying on transatlantic flights on TWA, BA or Virgin.

United Airlines Air Pass (in conjunction with any scheduled transatlantic carrier): Only the first flight needs to be pre-booked, all the rest can be left open:

	Low season	High season
Three coupons	$499	$479
Four coupons	$549	$579
Five coupons	$649	$679
Six coupons	$679	$709
Seven coupons	$709	$739
Eight coupons	$739	$769

One coupon = one flight; available for any flight on United's continental US network, but only one non-stop transcontinental flight is permitted between Boston, New York, Houston, Orlando, Miami, Philadelphia and Los Angeles, Phoenix, Seattle, San Francisco and San Diego. Valid for 60 days.

United Airlines Air Pass (in conjunction with the transatlantic flights of United Airlines, BA & Virgin):

	Low season	High season
Three coupons	£185	£205
Four coupons	£250	£270
Five coupons	£315	£335
Six coupons	£335	£355
Seven coupons	£355	£375
Eight coupons	£375	£395

One coupon = one flight. Valid for 60 days. Other rules as with previous air passes, however if transatlantic flight is with United, then two transcontinental journeys are allowed.

Delta Air Lines, American Airlines and Air Canada in conjunction with Continental Airlines, all operate similar confirmed reservation air passes on their respective networks. Their prices are similar to United's air pass rates.

America West Airlines (UK res 0483 440490):
Nationwide Pass: Valid for travel throughout the continental US, £59 per flight for a minimum of four flights; additional flights £37 per flight.
Tristate Pass: Valid for travel between California, Arizona and Nevada, £55 per flight for a minimum of two flights; additional flights £40 per flight.
Coast to Coast: £179 for two flights; valid for travel via Las Vegas or Phoenix between eastern and western continental US cities or vice versa (children 11 years and under, £145 per flight).

Buying the air pass
Work out the places in North America you wish to visit and see which airline's network of flights best matches your itinerary. An air pass trip around North America requires a lot of planning to be sure that you are getting the best value for your money. It's worth seeking the help of a specialist travel agent. These include STA Travel (071-581 1022); Trailfinders (071-938 3444) and Bon Voyage Travel (0703 330332).

US domestic airlines with UK offices
   Aloha Airlines (0273 722253)
   American West Airlines (0483 440490)
   American Airlines (081-577 4730)
   Continental Airlines (0293 771681)
   Delta Air Lines (0293 826100)
   Hawaiian Airlines (including MGM Grand Air, Heli USA, Lang Airlines) (0753 664406)
   Northwest Airlines (0293 574553)
   TWA (071-439 5947)
   United Airlines (081-750 9581)
   USAir (071-734 3001)

COACH TRAVEL

Those of a certain age will remember Paul Simon climbing aboard a bus in order 'to look for America' and Chuck Berry straddling a bus to get himself from Norfolk, Virginia to Los Angeles in 'Promised land'. If you want to sell chewing gum in a TV commercial, the sound of Free singing 'All right now' accompanied by pictures of a love-struck couple on an American Greyhound bus apparently conjures up the right image. Travelling by bus across America still resonates with romance.

The reality of bus travel, even in America, may often be less than romantic. Nevertheless for the family on a budget, a Greyhound bus pass remains the cheapest way of getting around. The buses are fairly comfortable: all coaches have air-conditioning, on-board toilets, reclining seats with head-rests and all buses are non-smoking. Many people save on a night's accommodation by sleeping on overnight journeys. Bus travel is also fairly safe (though to avoid problems you should sit up front nearer the driver). Seats are made available on a first-come, first-served basis, no advance reservations are possible – an eminently democratic arrangement.

The Greyhound bus Ameripass provides outstanding value. Fares start at £50 for a four-day ticket, which is valid for travel only on Monday to Thursdays. Children aged from 2-11 pay 50 per cent of the adult fare. A normal 7-day pass costs £85, a 15-day pass is £125 and a 30-day pass is £170. Again children aged 2-11 pay 50 per cent of the adult fare. Daily extensions, which must be purchased at the same time as the Ameripass ticket, cost £12 per day.

Further information: Greyhound International, Sussex House, London Road, East Grinstead, West Sussex RH19 1LD (0342 317317).

Rail Travel

The miracle of the American railway system is that despite the rise of the motor car and the boom in domestic air travel, it has managed to survive. And in common with many other countries (except Britain), rail travel is now enjoying something of a Renaissance in the States. High-speed trains have been tried out on journeys between Boston, New York and Washington DC. There is a plan to build a new fast-train link between Miami and Orlando in Florida.

Amtrak, the national rail company, which came into being in 1970 has done a creditable job of maintaining the network and promoting rail travel. Travelling on the train offers a double attraction. You pass through some extraordinary stations like Grand Central in New York and Union station in Washington, which are more like Renaissance cathedrals than transport terminals. And from the trains you see a fascinating slice of back-garden America.

It has to be said however that trains in America are fairly slow and outside the main commuter routes, operate a sparse timetable. Nevertheless the Amtrak unlimited travel passes offer superb value:

The National Pass: All Amtrak Routes: standard season 15 days £145; 30 days £215; peak season 15 days £215, 30 days £270.

The Western Pass: All routes west of Chicago and New Orleans: standard season 15 days £130, 30 days £180; peak season 15 days £160, 30 days £200.

The Eastern Pass: All routes east of Chicago and New Orleans: standard season 15 days £110, 30 days £145; peak season 15 days £125, 30 days £160.

The Far West Pass: All routes west of Denver and El Paso: standard season 15 days £110, 30 days £145; peak season 15 days £140, 30 days £160.

Coastal Pass: Montreal to Miami or Vancouver to San Diego: standard season 30 days £125; peak season 30 days £140.

Children under 16 pay 50 per cent; peak season rates apply from roughly the end of May to the end of August; sleeping berths can be obtained at extra cost.

Further information: Albany Tours, Royal London House, Second Floor, 196 Deansgate, Manchester M3 3NF (061-833 0202); Destination Marketing, 2 Cinnamon Row, Plantation Wharf, York Place, London SW11 3TW (071-978 5212); Explorers Tours, 223 Coppermill Road, Wraysbury, TW19 5NW (0753 681995); Thistle Air, 22 Bank Street, Kilmarnock, Ayrshire KA1 H1G (0563 31121).

CAR HIRE

Modern America is a country designed for people travelling in automobiles. Cities are planned for the car driver rather than the pedestrian. The family in America that does not have at least one car is an oddity. Cars are cheap and petrol (or 'gas' as it is called) is around 60p per gallon.

For any sort of holiday in America, a car is almost indispensable. A trip to Orlando and Disney World might not seem to require a car since you will be planning to spend most of your time in theme parks. Indeed it is possible to manage in Orlando by using taxis and shuttle buses, but your holiday will benefit immeasurably from being able to drive to and from the airport on arrival and departure – by being able to get yourself to the various attractions under your own steam. But perhaps the main argument to having a car is that driving in a car down the freeway with the air-conditioning going and the radio playing, you are enjoying the quintessential American experience.

Hiring a car however is not always as straightforward as it might seem. It can sometimes turn out to be a minefield of hazards for the unwary. Part of the problem is that everything is made to seem so straightforward – and so cheap. Fly/drive operators have brochures filled with 'bargain' offers for car rental, some promising 'free' weeks. If you decide to leave the hiring until you arrive in the States, you will be faced with an even wider array of special deals and prices offered by the many small local operators.

My recommendation is to arrange your car hire in this country, booking direct with one of the major hire companies. Most offer reduced rates such as Hertz's 'Affordable USA and Canada' which apply to rentals of at least three days if bookings are made in the UK at least 24 hours in advance. Another advantage is that you can pay for your car hire in advance, allowing you to budget for your travel arrangements more accurately.

But while American car hire companies promise an all-inclusive rate, when you arrive to pick your car up you might well find that it doesn't include all that it should. Unlimited mileage and loss damage waiver are normally included in the weekly rate but you will have to pay the local tax and you will be invited to take out LIS (Liability Insurance Supplement) which you should accept and Personal Accident Insurance which you should already have through your travel insurance policy. You may also be asked if you wish to pay for the full tank of petrol (so that you can bring it back empty). After years of grossly overcharging for petrol, US car hire companies have now taken to selling fuel at below market rates – so this is an offer worth accepting.

When you come to pick the car up you (and anybody else who

intends to drive) will need to produce a valid driving licence which has been held for a minimum of one year and a valid passport. The minimum age for renting a car is normally 21; for drivers aged 21-24 there is sometimes a surcharge.

When you hire a car in the States, plastic money is practically essential. It doesn't matter if you've paid in advance in the UK, the car hire desk in the States will demand an imprint from your card: either a credit card (Visa or Access) or charge card (American Express or Diners). They will probably accept a cash deposit covering the total estimated charges (together with your return airline ticket), but having a credit card is clearly the simpler option.

Remember speed limits are normally 55mph, but in some country areas on freeways, the limit has been increased to 65mph. The speed limits tend to be observed and are strictly enforced by the Highway Patrol who impose large on-the-spot fines. If you are stopped by a police car, remember that American policemen are justifiably jumpy. Do not suddenly get out of the car or make any other sudden movements. The Police are also strict on drinking and driving: even having a bottle of alcohol in a car is an offence in some states.

Avoid picking up your hired car after dark, straight after getting off your flight. Particularly in areas like Florida, where criminals prey on confused tourists, make arrangements to spend the night at an airport hotel and pick up your hired car in the morning.

When picking up your car, it is worth spending a short time checking it over carefully. American cars, even the medium-sized ones, are huge beasts. If you've never driven an automatic before, familiarize yourself with the controls. American cars don't have handbrakes, they have parking brakes which you operate with your left foot and release with your hand. You will only able to start the car when it's in 'P'; on some cars you will only be able to move the automatic control from 'P' (Park) to 'D' (Drive) via 'N' (Neutral) when you press the brake (the ordinary one, that is, not the foot/hand brake!).

When you start up don't press the accelerator too hard, let it move away as gently as possible. Remember that you will also have power steering as well as power brakes. You will also probably have a cruise control: when you switch it on and set the speed, the control will hold it at that speed without you keeping your foot on the accelerator. Touch the brake or the accelerator and the cruise control will automatically cut-out. Some cruise controls offer further refinements (such as 'resume' which allows you to drop speed temporarily before returning to your original pace). Given all these driver aids, it is easy to get the feeling that the car is driving itself.

While you can manage without cruise control, in any hot part of America (which means more or less all of America during the summer) air-conditioning is an indispensable item and definitely not a luxury. With air-conditioning, automatic transmission, power steering and wide, fast highways, long distances in America are fairly quick and easy to cover by car.

Before finally taking your car out of the car hire depot, give it a careful check over. If there is something wrong with it, it can save a lot of time and trouble if the problem is resolved before you set off. Even something as petty as a malfunctioning radio can be extremely annoying after a few days. Make sure the car has a spare tyre and a jack, and that you know how the jack works and how to open the bonnet (or 'hood' as it's called – the boot is the 'trunk').

If you've never driven a left-hand drive car before, or if you've never driven on the 'wrong' side of the road, have a short practice before you set off. The traffic travelling to and from most American airports frequently resembles the closing stages of the Indianapolis 500 motor race – you'll need all your wits about you. If you're preoccupied with looking for the light switch or you turn on the hazard warning lights when you want to indicate that you're switching lanes, you could quickly get yourself into trouble.

US car hire companies
Alamo Rent-a-car (0800 272200); Avis (081-848 8733); Bricar/Dollar (081-773 2321); Budget (0800 181181); Europcar (081-950 5050); Hertz (081-679 1799/0345 555888); Thrifty Car Rental (0494 474767).

Getting a car for free in the States
'Driveaway' agencies, situated in most American cities, are in business to find people to drive cars across the States while the cars' owners get to their destination by plane. For example, many New Yorkers spend the winter months in Florida but they don't want the trouble of driving their cars there and back. If the agency takes you on, you get a car free of charge for the journey – sometimes even free petrol.
Further information: Auto Driveaway, 310 South Michigan Avenue, Chicago, Illinois 60604 (312-939 3600) (UK office: PO Box 160, Ipswich, Suffolk IP1 1AD Tel: 0473 233748).

4

SELF-CATERING (AND HOUSE SWAPPING)

Compared with packages to Majorca or the Algarve, where self-catering accounts for over half of all holidays sold, relatively few British travellers to America contemplate the idea of renting an apartment or house.

For first-time visitors to the States, no doubt the prospect of having to fend for yourself might seem rather daunting. In fact, nothing could be further from the truth. Self-catering in America works as well as everything else works in the US. In fact having a large house or apartment at your disposal can be barely more expensive than having a room for a week in a medium-sized hotel – with the advantage of staying in somewhere with more space and added facilities like washing machines.

In Orlando, where the self-catering concept is at its most developed, the choice of self-catering is huge. From modest-sized studio apartments with kitchenettes to full-blown four-bedroom houses with heated pools, double garages, laundry rooms and cable TV with access to 50 channels.

The problem is finding out what sort of self-catering properties are available at your chosen destination. With the exception of Orlando and the rest of Florida – and more recently, New England – UK operators do very little to promote self-catering packages to the States. If you can't find any suitable ideas from our list of operators below, the best alternative is to look at the list of hotel operators in chapter 5: most of the main chains now have properties with some degree of self-catering, with suites that have kitchens and sitting rooms. You could also contact the local tourist office for your chosen destination and ask them to send you details of local agencies that offer properties for short-term holiday rental.

Eating out

Self-catering in America will still probably involve a substantial amount of eating out since restaurants and other eating places in America offer such outstanding value. Whenever we self-cater in America, we have a breakfast and one other meal during the day in the rented house, but eat one meal out. The attraction of eating in is not so much cost (though given the low prices in American supermarkets, you can still save money by eating at home), it is the convenience. If you have spent a hard day at a theme park, for example, it is nice to come home and flop in front of the television and cook up a frozen pizza or some pasta.

Tour operators offering self-catering packages

California

Jetsave (0342 312033)
Villas in the Palm Desert region of Palm Springs. Prices start from £465 per person for seven nights, flight inclusive.
North America Travel Service (0532 432525)
Palm Springs and Newport Beach. Prices on application.

Colorado

Crystal Holidays (081-399 5144)
Pine Ridge Condominiums in Breckenridge with open log fires, cable TVs and two bathrooms in each unit cost from £409 to £565 per person for seven nights. This price includes a return airfare to Denver from Gatwick and car hire.
Peregor Travel (0895 639900)
Houses, condominiums and apartments in Breckenridge, Vail and Beaver Creek. A three-bedroom house in Breckenridge, for example, costs from £499 to £645 per property, for seven nights.

Florida

America Ad Lib (0732 867300)
Private villas and apartments in Orlando, Key West, Sanibel Island and Sarasota. For example, a week in a three-bedroom unit in Key West costs £895. This price is for the rental of the apartment only.
Bon Voyage (0703 330332)
Villas and apartments in the Kissimmee area of Orlando and the Gulf Coast. A three-bedroom villa in Orlando which sleeps up to seven people costs £399 for seven nights. The supplement for a private pool is £90 for seven nights.
British Airways Holidays (0293 617000)
Orlando – villas with pools and apartments. A two-bedroom villa with a private pool, sleeping six people, costs from £485 to £805 per person for seven nights, flight inclusive.
Falcon (061-745 7000)
Orlando and the Gulf Coast. For example, a fortnight at the Isla

Bahia del Mar luxury homes in St Petersburg costs from £399 to £729 per person, based on four adults sharing a two-bedroom apartment.

Flightbookers (071-757 2000)

Orlando: a seven-night stay in a villa with a private pool costs from £539 to £693 per person. This price includes accommodation, flights and car hire plus insurance.

Florida Homes and Apartments (021-323 2413)

Apartments and homes in all the popular areas of Florida. For example, a three-bedroom home in Key West costs from £689 per week. A two-bedroom apartment in Orlando costs from £299 per week.

Florida Vacations (0727 841568)

Villas and apartments in Orlando, Sarasota, St Petersburg area, Sanibel, Captiva and North Captiva Island, the upper Keys and Key West. One week in a two-storey stilt home, sleeping six people, on Captiva Island with your own private board walk to the beach costs from £595 to £1645. This price is for accommodation only and excludes the cost of travelling to the States.

Hermis Travel (071-731 3979)

Apartments in Orlando and the Gulf Coast. Two centre holidays are also offered. For example, 14 nights at Fantasy World Villas in Kissimmee, three miles from Disney World, costs from £587 to £773 per person, based on four sharing. This price includes return flights from Gatwick.

Jetlife Holidays (0322 614801)

Apartments, villas and luxury homes in Orlando, Longboat Key, Sanibel Island, Captiva Island and North Redington Beach. A two-bedroom home in Orlando costs from £369 per person for seven nights, excluding airfare.

Jetsave (0342 312033)

Villas and apartments in Miami, Orlando, the Keys, Fort Myers and the Gulf Coast. For example, a week's stay on the Gulf Coast, at the Aloha Bay Apartments – a Polynesian theme apartment complex, with a freshwater swimming pool and a private dock, costs from £255 to £345 per apartment. Flights are not included.

Key to America (0784 248777)

Luxury homes located in Kissimmee, approximately five miles from Disney World and apartments in Orlando. Villas, condominiums and two- and three-bedroom apartments are also available on the Gulf Coast. Fourteen nights in a four-bedroom villa in Kissimmee, sleeping eight adults costs from £412 to £585 per person, flight inclusive. This price also includes car hire.

Meon Travel (0730 268411)

Luxury, privately-owned villas, mostly with their own swimming pools in the Kissimmee, Gulf Coast and Longboat Key areas of

Florida. Two weeks at a three-bedroomed villa with private pool in Kissimmee costs from £673 per person. Prices include scheduled flights from London Gatwick, car hire and welcome food hamper.

N.A.R.(UK) Ltd (0753 855031)
Apartments in Orlando from $750 (£500) to $1120 (£746) per week for a unit sleeping up to six people.

North America Travel Service (0532 432525)
Orlando and Newport Richey: two weeks at a three-bedroom home in Orlando costs from £492 to £679 per person, based on six sharing and including flights.

North American Vacations (091-483 6226)
Villas, apartments and private house rentals in Orlando. A three-bedroom house with a private pool costs from $819 (£546) to $888 (£592) per week, excluding airfare.

Owners Abroad (0293 554444)
A two-bedroom apartment on the Isla del Sol, St Petersburg costs from £345 to £445 per person, based on six adults sharing, flight inclusive.

Peregor Travel (0895 639900)
Villas and apartments in Orlando and on the Gulf Coast. For example, seven nights at a two-bedroom apartment on the Gulf Coast at Indian Shores costs from £349 to £565 per property.

Premier Holidays (0223 355977)
Destinations featured include Orlando, St Petersburg, Longboat Key, Sanibel and Captiva Islands. Accommodation ranges from apartments to houses with private pools. One week at a four-bedroom house in Orlando costs from £407 to £474 per person, including return scheduled flights and a car for seven days.

Something Special Travel (0992 586999)
Destinations include Orlando, or on the coast in Hudson, New Port Richey, Tarpon Springs, Clearwater, St Petersburg, Sarasota, Longboat Key, Siesta Key, St Armands Key, Lido Key, Sanibel, Captiva, Naples and Marco Island. Two weeks for a family of four in the Orlando area costs from £547 to £678 per person, including flights. Two weeks on Longboat Key for a family of four costs from £681 to £800 per person, including flights.

Thomas Cook (0733 68519)
Kissimmee, Orlando – from two-bedroom town houses to three-bedroom family homes. Prices range from £51 to £83 per night for a two-bedroom villa sleeping six people.

Travelcoast (081-891 2222)
Private villas, condominium resorts and apartments in many areas of Florida. For example, a two-bedroom unit at the Blue Tree Resort in Orlando costs from £87 per day.

Travelpack (061-707 4404)
Locations include Orlando, the Gulf Coast, the East Coast and central Florida. For example, a week in an apartment at Isla del Sol in St Petersburg which sleeps up to six people, costs from £450 to £665. This price is per property.

Ultimate Holidays (0279 755527)
Houses and condominiums in Orlando. Seven nights in a two-bedroom condominium costs from £405 to £525 per person, flight inclusive.

Unijet Travel (0444 459191)
Orlando, the Gulf Coast, Sanibel and Captiva Islands and Longboat Key. For example, a week in a two-bedroom apartment at the Vistana Resort in Orlando costs from £679 to £729. This price is for the apartment per week and includes a rental-free car. Accommodation can only be booked in conjunction with Unijet flights.

Virgin Holidays (0293 617181)
A seven-night stay at the Famous Host Inn in Orlando costs from £389 to £579 per person, including flights and car hire.

New England

New England Country Homes (0328 856666)
Maine, New Hampshire, Vermont, Massachusetts and Connecticut. For example, a two-week holiday on Martha's Vineyard, staying in a wood-shingled cottage less than a mile from the sea, costs from £742 to £903 per person, based on four sharing. This price includes flights, car hire and first night hotel stop-over.

New England Inns and Resorts (0923 821469)
All types and category of accommodation is offered by this booking service. An administrative charge of between £75 and £100 per holiday is made, depending on the amount of time spent planning the trip with the client. Payment for the accommodation is made to the individual properties. The price range for the property rental is between £800 and £3800, excluding airfare.

United States: more than one state

America Ad Lib (0732 867300)
American Dream offers villas and apartments in Florida and Hawaii. Prices range from £500 per person, in Florida for six sharing.

North American Vacations (091-483 6226)
Condo's and villas in Florida and Hawaii. Prices for two weeks, including return air travel from Gatwick or Heathrow, range from £500 to £3000 per person.

HOUSE SWAPPING

One of the most difficult problems about holidays is finding the right accommodation, particularly if you have children. Not only are hotels or self-catering apartments rarely suitable or particularly comfortable for families, they hardly ever offer a genuine view of life in the place where you are staying.

Wouldn't it be much better to stay in a real home on holiday, to have the normal comforts and luxuries of domestic life: a washing machine, proper-sized rooms and a fully-equipped kitchen? And to stay amongst real people, not other holidaymakers from your own country?

One answer is house swapping; exchanging your home for a couple of weeks or more with another family. With an exchange, not only will you get the use of the other family's house, and perhaps also their car, you will also gain admission to the local community.

It seems a good idea, but what of the pitfalls? How do you find people to swap with, how do you arrange the swap, how can you be sure your house will be looked after properly, does your home insurance cover such exchanges?

How to swap

The most straightforward way to arrange an overseas or UK swap is to advertise, for a fee, in a house-swapping directory: the biggest is produced by Intervac. Several directories are published in Britain:

Home Base Holidays, 7 Park Avenue, London N13 5PG (081-886 8752): Specializes in home swaps with families in the US and Canada. It produces three brochures a year; membership costs £32.

Homelink International, Linfield House, Gorse Hill Road, Virginia Water, Surrey GU25 4AS (0344 842642): One of the biggest home-swapping agencies with more than 16,000 registered members in over 50 countries, it publishes six catalogues during the year; annual membership £47.

Intervac International Home Exchange, 3 Orchard Court, North Wraxall, Chippenham, Wiltshire SN14 7AD (0225 982208): Over 9,000 members and three directories a year (with a late-exchange service). Annual membership is £65.

You could also consider trying to arrange a swap through personal contacts: friends or friends of friends who live overseas. If the company you work for, for example, has overseas offices and representatives, perhaps you might be able to organize a swap through them.

43

The possible dangers

According to the home-swapping agencies, home swapping disasters hardly ever happen: the only problem is likely to be that the person you're planning to swap with has to back out because of family illness or the death of a relative.

The agencies report that families are very good about paying for any breakages or any damage they cause. Intervac says the fact that there is no rental fee involved seems to make people especially careful about how they treat the house where they are unminded guests. But if you are especially house-proud however then house swapping may not suit you. If you wish to swap your house, it helps if it is a place well known as a tourist area: in London, for example, or Oxford – but location isn't always important.

Insurance: You must tell your house and car insurance company about the exchange: if you don't, it may affect your cover.

Further information: The Consumers Association magazine *Which?* (November 1986) has a very useful guide to house swapping, and advice on making the necessary arrangements. Back numbers of *Which?* are available from reference libraries.

5

HOTELS AND MOTELS

We British have never been entirely comfortable with the idea of spending time in hotels. Our diffidence is understandable. For the most part British hotels have tended to be been too expensive and far too uncomfortable (and cheap bed and breakfast places were too cheap and too nasty). Those in the hotel business knew that Basil Fawlty and Fawlty Towers were nearer fact than fiction.

The Americans however are great hotel and motel users. The rise of the automobile in the fifties and the boom in air travel in the sixties, helped create a new generation of Americans who were always on the move and forever on the lookout for somewhere cheap and cheerful to stay. The rise of chains like Holiday Inn and Hilton created a new breed of hotel and motel: smart establishments that offered good minimum standards of service at a very competitive price. They might be homogenously bland but in hotels people took this as a prized quality (the alternative was probably highly individual establishments overrun by cockroaches and vermin).

Whether you want a stay-put holiday or a driving tour through America, one thing you can be sure of is finding good accommodation at bargain prices. Rates tend to be flexible, fixed according to supply and demand. In places like Orlando, New York and Los Angeles with a high conglomeration of accommodation, competition is knife-sharp. Drive down International Drive in Orlando, for example, and you will see the hotels and motels displaying their current rates on electronic display boards. And not only cheap rates but offers for free breakfasts or free in-room movies.

For the lodging industry the quiet days are at the weekend: Friday, Saturday and Sunday nights when business travellers are at home with their nearest and dearest. All American hotels offer some sort of special weekend-break rate.

Whether at weekends or during the week, if you don't see a special deal advertised, ask (ask anyway). Haggling is common. If you are embarrassed to do it face to face, do it by phone. 'I'm looking for a room tonight for three nights.' 'Our rate is $65 per night plus tax.' 'I was looking for something a little cheaper.' 'I can offer you our Great Escape package: two nights including breakfast for $99.95.' 'What about three nights?' 'I can offer you three nights for $150...'. By using the phone you can telephone several establishments, compare prices and play one place off against each other. No American hotel is ever knowingly undersold.

A growing trend in the hotel and motel business is a switch towards self-catering. Places like Days' Lodges and Marriott's Residence Inns offer bedrooms, sitting rooms and small kitchens with microwave ovens, freezers and all utensils where you can prepare your own food. Eating out in America is cheap but preparing your own meals works out even cheaper (the wide-open spaces of American supermarkets, the amply stocked shelves and the bargain prices are a revelation).

Prices for 'residences' and 'conveniences' are generally open to negotiation. Remember, if you don't ask you won't get.

Hotel passes and vouchers

A number of schemes are available allowing you to pre-buy hotel accommodation before you arrive in America. This has the advantage of allowing you to plan your holiday budget more exactly, but it has the disadvantage of limiting you to one particular hotel group (of course, if you are happy with that hotel group this is not a disadvantage). The main problem might be that you want to stay in a place that either has no hotel of your chosen group – or where the hotel of your chosen group is full.

The Days Inn (0483 440470) 'Go As you Please' Hotel Pass covers four price bands: from £33 per night to £63 per night, depending on the particular hotel. The new Days Inn in Manhattan, for example is in the Gold Category, which costs £63 per night (plus a £20 supplement) including tax – a reasonable price for a room for four people.

Howard Johnson Hotels, Suites & Lodges and Ramada Hotels: Combine to offer the Freedom Hotel Pass (sold in the UK by Travel & Tourism Marketing, tel: 081-688 1418). There are over 800 hotels participating in the scheme: travellers must purchase a minimum of three vouchers. Vouchers cost from £29 to £95 per night depending on the grade of hotel.

Discover America Marketing (0992 441517): Offers the Discover America Hotel Pass which covers 400 hotels and motels of the following chains: Vagabond Inns, La Quinta Inns, Hampton Inns and other selected independent hotels. The rate of $59.50 (£39.50) per room per night covers up to four people and provides free continental breakfast in Vagabond, La Quinta and Hampton Inns.

American Hotel and Motel Chains with UK offices

Best Western, Vine House, 143 London Road, Kingston upon Thames, Surrey KT2 6NA (081-541 0033).

Choice Hotels International, 2 Valentine Place, London SE1 8QH (071-928 3333): Bookings for Quality Inns, Comfort Inns, Sleep Inns, Clarion Hotels, Friendship, Rodeway Inns, Econolodge.

Days Inn of America, 2 The Billings, Walnut Tree Close, Guildford, Surrey GU1 4YD (0483 440470).

Discover America Marketing Group, The Priests House, 90 High Road, Broxbourne EN10 7DZ (0992 441517): Bookings for La Quinta, Radisson Hotels, Vagabond Inns, Embassy Suites, Inns of North America and Hampton Inns.

Hilton Hotels Corporation, The Chambers, Suite 105/106, Chelsea Harbour, London SW10 0XG (071-376 4848).

Holiday Inns Worldwide, Bridge Street, Banbury, Oxfordshire OX16 8RQ (0295 272278).

Howard Johnson Hotels, c/o Travel & Tourism Marketing (North America), 20 Barclay Road, Croydon, Surrey CR0 1JN (081-688 1418).

Hyatt Hotels & Resorts, 113 Upper Richmond Road, London SW15 2TL (081-780 1000).

Inter-Continental Hotels Group, Intercontinental House, The Thameside Centre, Kew Bridge Road, Brentford TW8 0EB (081-847 3711).

Marriott Hotels, Quadrant House, 80 Regent Street, London W1R 6AQ (071-439 0281).

New England Inns & Resorts, 1 Farm Way, Northwood HA6 3EG (09238 21469).

Ramada Inns c/o Travel & Tourism Marketing (North America), 20 Barclay Road, Croydon, Surrey CR0 1JN (081-688 1418/0800 181737).

Rodeway Inns c/o Travel & Tourism Marketing (North America), 20 Barclay Road, Croydon, Surrey CR0 1JN (081-688 1418).

Sheraton, The Kiln House, 210 New Kings Road, London SW6 4NZ (0800 353535).

Travelodge, Gatehouse Industrial Estate, Aylesbury, HP19 3EB (0296 432 861).

Westin Hotels & Resorts, 7/8 Conduit Street, London SW1R 9TG (071-408 0636).

Budget Motel Chains

('800' telephone numbers are free phone numbers which can only be dialled from within the US.)

Best Inns of America, PO Box 1719, Marion, IL 62959-7719 (618-997 5454 / 800-237 8466).

Budget Host Inns, PO Box 10656, Fort Worth TX 76114 (817-957 4200 / 800-283 4678).

Budgetel Inns, 212 West Wisconsin Avenue, Milwaukee, WI 53203 (800-428 3438).

Comfort Inns, 10750 Columbia Pike, Silver Spring MD 20901-4494 (414-272 8484 / 800-221 2222).

Days Inns of America, 339 Jefferson Rd, Parsippany, NJ 07054-0278 (404-329 7466 / 800-375 2525).

Drury Inns, 10801 Pear Tree Lane, St Ann, MO 63074 (314-429 2255 / 800-325 8300).

EZ 8 Motels, 2484 Hotel Circle Plaza, San Diego, CA 92108 (619-291 4824 / 800-326 6835).

Econo Lodges of America, 10750 Columbia Pike, Silver Spring, MD 20901-4494 (301-593 5600 / 800-446 6900).

Economy Inns of America, 5367 West Irlo Bronson Memorial Highway, Kissimmee, FL 34746 (619-438 6661 / 800-826 0778)

Exel Inns of America, 4706 East Washington Avenue, Madison, WI 53704 (608-241 5271 / 800-241 5271)

Friendship Inns Hotel Corporation, 10750 Columbia Pike, Silver Spring, MD 20901-4494 (301-593 5600 / 800-453 4511).

Hampton Inns, 6800 Poplar Avenue, Suite 200, Memphis, TN 38138 (901-768 3100 / 800-426 7866).

Hojo Inns Howard Johnson, 339 Jefferson Road, Parsippany, NJ 07054-0278 (800-446 4656).

Knight's Inns, 26650 Emery Parkway, Cleveland, OH 44128 (614-755 6230 / 800-722 7220).

Motel 6, 14651 Dallas Parkway, Suite 500, Dallas, TX 75240 (505-891 6161).

Red Carpet Inns, 1152 Spring Street, Suite A, Atlanta, GA 30309 (404-873 5924 / 800-251 1962).

Red Roof Inns, 4355 Davidson Road, Hilliard, OH 43026-9699 (614-876 3200 / 800-843 7663).

Scottish Inns, 1152 Spring Street, Suite A, Atlanta, GA 30309 (404-873 5924 / 800-251 1962).

Select Inns of America, PO Box 9080, Fargo, ND 58106 (800-641 1000).

Super 8 Motels, PO Box 4090, Aberdeen, SD 57402 -4090 (605-225 2272 / 800-800 8000).

Suisse Chalet, Chalet Drive, Wilton, NH 03086-0657 (800-524 2358).

Travelodge, Forte Hotels Reservation Center, 1973 Friendship Drive, El Cajon, CA 92020 (619-448 1884 / 800 255 3050).

Also worth considering:
Allstar Inns (805-687 3383)
Arborgate Inns (614-755 6230)
Best Western (602-957 4200 / 800-528 1234)
Choice Hotels (301-593 5600 / 800-424 4777)
Clarion (301-593 5600 / 800-424 4777)
Cross Country Inns (614-766 0037 / 800-621 1429)
Independent Motels of America (605-842 3418 / 800-341 8000)
La Quinta Motor Inn (512-366 6000 / 800-531 5900)
McIntosh Motor Inns (215-279 6000)
Master Host Inns (404-873 5924 / 800-251 1962)
Microtel (716-436 6000 / 800-365 6835)
Quality Inns (301-593 5600)
Rodeway Inns (800-221 2222)
Shoney's Inns (800-222 2222)
Sleep Inn (301-593 5600 / 800-627 5227)

HOTEL HOLIDAYS

All over America

America Ad Lib (0732 867300)
Single- and multi-centre holidays or combination air tours. For example a seven-night stay at the Sheraton Hotel on Key Largo in Florida costs from £529 to £909 per person, based on two sharing, including flights and car hire.
American Connections (0494 473173)
Up-market accommodation across America. For example a stay at the Arizona Biltmore in Phoenix, Arizona costs from £61 to £123 per night, per room, based on two people sharing.
American Dream (081-470 1181)
Resort hotels in Florida, Phoenix, Tucson, Las Vegas, Los Angeles, San Diego, San Francisco, Santa Barbara, Carmel and Hawaii. A seven-night stay at the Hyatt Islandia in San Diego, for example, costs from £205 per person. A hotel voucher programme in conjunction with hotel groups Howard Johnson, Ramada and Days Inn also operates, which offers over 1,000 locations throughout the USA. Days Inn vouchers range from £29 to £55 per night, per room. Reservations for rooms can be made in advance by ringing a UK number.
Frontiers Travel (081-742 1488)
Planned itineraries and pre-booked accommodation across America. For example, an 11-day California Wanderer which includes overnight stays in San Francisco, Lake Tahoe, Yosemite National Park, Monterey, San Simeon and Los Angeles costs

around £276 per person, based on two adults sharing. Flights are not included. Pre-booked accommodation starts at around £50 per night for a twin-bedded room.

Hermis Travel (071-731 3979)
A choice of hotels in Hawaii, Los Angeles, San Francisco, Phoenix, Tucson, Las Vegas, Reno, Lake Tahoe, Denver, Charleston, Myrtle Beach, New Orleans, Palm Springs, San Diego and throughout Florida. For example, seven nights at the Best Western Timber Cove Lodge on Lake Tahoe costs from £582 to £726 per person, flight inclusive. This price also includes free car hire. Twin- and multi-centre holidays are also available. For instance, a trip combining New York and Florida, spending two nights in Niagara, five nights in New York and seven nights in Orlando costs from £880 to £895 per person, flight inclusive.

Jetsave (0342 312033)
Fourteen- and seventeen-night holidays 'touring by air' to major tourist destinations. For example, the Golden Triangle tour visits San Francisco, Las Vegas and Los Angeles and costs from £719 to £885 per person. This price includes all hotel accommodation, return transatlantic flights and scheduled flights within the USA.

Jetset Tours (061 953 0920)
All major cities in America. Prices range from £17 in the Days Inn, Orlando to £99 in The Pierre, New York. All prices are per person, per night.

N.A.R.(UK) Ltd (0753 855031)
Accommodation in cities in all states. For example, a twin room at the Hilton in Anchorage, Alaska costs from $119 to $279 per night.

North America Travel Service (0532 432525)
First class, luxury resort and city hotels throughout all 50 states. For example, seven nights in Tucson costs from £589 to £677 per person, including flights.

North American Vacations (091-483 6226)
Over 2,000 hotel, motel and resort properties in over 350 cities, towns, villages and resorts. All hotel rates are per room, per night inclusive of all local taxes. For example, a twin room in the Comfort Inn in Key West, Florida costs from $89 (£57) to $135 (£90). A twin room in the Colonial Inn in Martha's Vineyard, Massachusetts costs from $86 to $155.

Peregor Travel (0895 639900)
Hotels of all categories in cities and resorts. A choice of two- and three-centre holidays is offered. For example, a seven-night holiday in South Carolina at the Westin Resort Hilton Head Island costs from £475 to £789 per person. This price includes return mid-week flights, accommodation and seven days' car rental.

Premier Holidays (0223 355977)
A range of accommodation is offered, in all price ranges. A seven-

night room-only package at the Ramada Inn Disneyland costs from £445 to £722 per person, including return airfare to San Francisco from London.

Arizona

Key to America (0784 248777)
Accommodation offered in Scottsdale. For example, a week's stay at the Scottsdale Princess Hotel, which is a Spanish-style resort property costs from £572 to £879 per person, flight inclusive. This price includes car hire with unlimited mileage.
Kuoni Travel (0306 742222)
Scottsdale: seven nights at the Scottsdale Plaza, a Mediterranean-style, first class hotel, costs from £530 to £639 per person, flight inclusive.

California

Bon Voyage (0703 330332)
A 10-day California Wanderer self-drive tour takes in San Francisco, Santa Rosa, Lake Tahoe, Yosemite National Park, Monterey, San Simeon and Los Angeles. The price between April and October is £265 per person, based on two adults sharing a room. Airfares and car hire are not included.
Flightbookers (071-757 2000)
San Diego, Anaheim, Los Angeles and San Francisco: a seven-night stay at the Inn at the Park in Anaheim costs from £439 to £579 per person, based on two sharing. This price includes accommodation, flights and car hire plus insurance.
Funway Holidays (081-466 0222)
Los Angeles, San Francisco, San Diego and Monterey. Seven nights at the Bahia Resort Hotel in San Diego costs from £549 to £749 per person, flight inclusive.
Jetlife Holidays (0322 614801)
Destinations include Los Angeles, San Diego and San Francisco. Seven nights in a superior grade hotel in Los Angeles costs from £549 to £819 per person, flight inclusive.
Key to America (0784 248777)
Accommodation offered in Los Angeles, San Francisco and San Diego. For example a week's stay at the Hyatt Fisherman's Wharf, near to Pier 39 and Ghirardelli Square costs from £582 to £752 per person, flight inclusive.
Page & Moy (0533 524433)
The Golden Triangle Tour: this combines Los Angeles, San Francisco and Las Vegas for either 11 or 14 nights. Prices range from £750 to £900 per person for the 11-night option. This price

includes air travel and accommodation.
Peltours (081-346 9144)
Destinations include Los Angeles, San Francisco and San Diego. For example, a seven-night stay at the Beverley Hilton in Los Angeles, costs from £690 to £961 per person, flight inclusive.
Unijet Travel (0444 459191)
One- or two-centre holidays and three- and four-centre air tours. For example, a three-centre Great Western air tour visiting Los Angeles, San Francisco, San Diego and Las Vegas costs from £969 to £1115 per person for 14 nights. This price includes flights, accommodation and breakfast every day.
Virgin Holidays (0293 617181)
All over California. A seven-night stay at the Seapoint Hotel in San Diego costs from £509 to £639 per person, flight inclusive. A seven-night stay at the Carmel Mission Inn in Monterey costs from £559 to £689 per person, including flights.

Colorado

Crystal Holidays (081-399 5144)
Hotels, inns and lodges in Breckenridge and Vail. Seven nights in the four-star Beaver Run Hotel, costs from £509 to £654 per person. This price includes return airfare to Denver and free car hire.

Florida

Bon Voyage (0703 330332)
Orlando, the Gulf Coast, Sanibel Island, Naples, Miami Beach and the Keys. A stay at the Hampton Inn at Key West costs £49 per room, per night. A room at the West Wind Inn on Sanibel Island costs £65 per night.
British Airways Holidays (0293 617000)
Orlando, the Gulf Coast and the Gold Coast. For example, a 14-night holiday at the Orlando Marriott, set in 48 acres of water-scaped grounds and 25 minutes away from the Magic Kingdom costs from £649 to £974 per person, based on two sharing, flight inclusive. Two-centre holidays are also offered, for instance seven nights in Orlando combined with seven nights in the Florida Keys costs from £742 to £1298 per person, based on two sharing, flight inclusive.
Falcon (061-745 7000)
Orlando and the Gulf Coast. For example, a 14-night holiday at the Hotel Langford resort in Winter Park, Orlando costs from £415 to £665 per person, based on two sharing. Twin-centre holidays in Orlando and the Gulf Coast are also offered.

Flightbookers (071-757 2000)
Orlando, Miami and Key West. A seven-night holiday at the Grosvenor Resort in Orlando costs from £560 to £705 per person, based on two sharing. This price includes accommodation, flights and one week's car hire plus insurance.

Funway Holidays (081-466 0222)
Orlando, Clearwater, St Petersburg, Fort Myers, Sarasota, Naples, Marco Beach, Miami Beach, Key West, Fort Lauderdale, Palm Beach and Cocoa Beach. Seven nights at the Naples Beach Hotel and Golf Club, for example, costs from £515 to £649 per person, flight inclusive.

Jetlife Holidays (0322 614801)
All standards of hotel in Orlando, Treasure Island, St Petersburg, Clearwater, Sarasota Keys, Fort Myers, Naples, Hollywood, Fort Lauderdale, Sunny Isles and Key West. Seven nights at the Quality Inn International in Orlando costs from £465 to £585 per person. This price includes flights and car hire.

Jetsave (0342 312033)
Destinations include Orlando, St Petersburg, Clearwater, Sarasota, Fort Myers, Miami, Fort Lauderdale and the Keys. For example, 14 nights at the Holiday Inn, on the island of Longboat Key, Sarasota, costs from £735 to £839 per person, based on two sharing. The price includes flights and car hire.

Key to America (0784 248777)
Accommodation offered in Orlando, the Gulf Coast, Miami, Fort Lauderdale, Palm Beach and the Keys. For example, a week's stay at the Hawk's Cay Resort and Marina at Duck Key, which is located on its own 60-acre island, 45 minutes south of Key Largo and one hour north of Key West costs from £575 to £809 per person, flight inclusive. This price also includes car hire with unlimited mileage.

Kuoni Travel (0306 742222)
Holidays in Orlando, the Gulf Coast, the South Coast and The Keys. For example, seven nights at the Boca Raton Beach Club costs from £770 to £1043 per person, flight inclusive.

Lotus Supertravel (071-962 9933)
Resort holidays on the Keys or the Gulf Coast islands of Sanibel or Captiva. A seven-night holiday costs from £259 per person.

N.A.R.(UK) Ltd (0753 855031)
All categories of hotel throughout the state. For example, hotel rooms in Fort Myers range in price from $32 (£21) to $77 (£51) per person, based on two sharing.

Northwest Airlines (0424 732777)
Inclusive packages to Orlando or the Gulf Coast. For example, seven nights in the Ramada Resort, three miles from Disney World costs from £449 to £640 per person, based on two people

sharing. Prices include airfares and car rental.

Owners Abroad (0293 554444)
Orlando and the Gulf Coast. For example, two weeks at the Ramada Inn, Orlando costs from £355 to £419 per person, including flights and car hire.

Peltours (081-346 9144)
Destinations include Sand Key in the Tampa Bay area, Clearwater, Sanibel Island, Sarasota, Naples, Orlando, Fort Lauderdale and Miami Beach. For example, seven nights on Sanibel Island, on the Gulf Coast, at the Sundial Beach and Tennis resort costs from £760 to £1329 per person, based on mid-week British Airways flights to Miami. Prices also include accommodation and car hire.

Sunworld (0532 393020)
Orlando plus two-centre holidays which combine Orlando with Fort Lauderdale or the Gulf Coast. For example, a seven-night stay at the Orlando Marriott on International Drive, costs from £529 to £689 per person, flight inclusive. Children's prices start at £199.

Transamerica (0293 774441)
Accommodation in Orlando, the Northern Gulf beaches, Sanibel and Captiva, Naples and Marco Island, the Atlantic beaches and the Keys. A week's stay at the Radisson Suite Resort which is an all-suites hotel situated on the beach of Marco Island costs from £489 to £799 per person, flight inclusive. Fourteen nights in Orlando at the Quality Inn, Kissimmee, situated four and a half miles from Disney World costs from £499 to £629 per person, flight inclusive, based on two sharing.

Transolar Travel (051-630 3737)
Cocoa Beach, Orlando, Miami Beach, Clearwater, St Petersburg and Hollywood Beach. For example, two weeks at the Doubletree Club Hotel in Orlando, costs from £616 per person, based on two sharing. A fortnight at the Orlando Vacation Resort costs from £387 per person, based on four sharing a room. These prices include flights, accommodation and a rental car with unlimited mileage.

Travelpack (061-707 4404)
Locations include Kissimmee, Orlando, the Gulf Coast, the East Coast and central Florida. For example, a week at the Hyatt Orlando costs from £320 to £380 per room which sleeps up to four people.

Ultimate Holidays (0279 755527)
Orlando, the Gulf Coast, Key Largo, Key West and the Gold Coast. For instance, a 14-night holiday at the Holiday Inn Ocean Club and Marina in Fort Lauderdale on the east coast costs from £599 to £759 per person, based on two sharing, flight inclusive. Flights are from Manchester or Gatwick.

Unijet Travel (0444 459191)
Orlando as a one-centre holiday or combined with St Petersburg, Clearwater, North Redington, Longboat Key, Miami, Fort Lauderdale or Key West. For example, a two-week stay in Orlando and Clearwater costs from £769 to £929 per person, flight inclusive. This price also includes a rental-free car.

Hawaii

Bon Voyage (0703 330332)
Five nights' accommodation at the Outrigger Prince Kuhio hotel in Waikiki costs £225 per person. The price includes a lei greeting at the airport, an island tour by mini-coach and a luau feast. A stay in Hawaii can easily be added on to a Californian holiday.

Hawaiian Travel Centre (071-706 4142)
A one-centre holiday in Waikiki for 14 nights costs from £1070 to £1215 per person, based on two sharing a first class hotel room. An island-hopping holiday which spends four nights in Oahu, four nights in Maui, five nights in Kauai and five nights in Hawaii costs from £1240 to £1370 per person based on two sharing a budget hotel room. A west coast USA and Hawaii holiday which spends four nights in San Francisco, three nights in Waikiki and three nights in Los Angeles costs from £1960 to £2100 per person, based on two sharing a deluxe hotel room. All prices include return flights.

Jetsave (0342 312033)
Seven nights on Waikiki Beach costs from £799 to £939 per person, based on two sharing. Prices include return flights.

Jetset Tours (061-953 0920)
Holidays in solely Hawaii or combined with California. For example, a seven-night stay on Oahu in Hilton hotels costs from £799 to £949 per person, flight inclusive.

Key to America (0784 248777)
Accommodation offered on Oahu, Maui, Kauai and Hawaii. For example, a week's stay at the Prince Kuhio Hotel on Waikiki Beach costs from £749 to £882 per person, flight inclusive.

Kuoni Travel (0306 742222)
Oahu, Maui, Kauai and Hawaii. One and two island holidays are offered. For example, seven nights at the Pacific Beach Hotel on Waikiki combined with seven nights at the Sheraton Kauai costs from £1155 to £1236 per person, flight inclusive. Extensions to Hawaii can be added to any holiday that ends in Los Angeles.

Page & Moy (0533 524433)
Fourteen or twenty-one nights on the island of Oahu, staying in the Waikiki resort, costs from £859 to £1085 per person, including airfare. The third week is free. It is also possible to combine a

week on the West Coast with a week in Hawaii. This costs from £899 per person, air inclusive.

Transamerica (0293 774441)
Hotels in Kauai, Maui, Hawaii and Oahu. A three-night stay at the five-star Hotel Sheraton Hana on the east coast of Maui staying in one-storey plantation-style cottages costs around £379 per person, accommodation only.

Unijet Travel (0444 459191)
One-centre and island-hopping holidays. For example a four-centre holiday, visiting Waikiki, Maui and Kauai with one night either end in Los Angeles costs from £1359 to £1549 per person, flight inclusive.

United Vacations (081-313 0999)
Oahu, Maui, Kauai and Hawaii. For example, seven nights at the Sheraton Waikiki Hotel on Oahu costs from £808 to £972 per person. This price includes flights and accommodation. Island-hopping holidays are also offered.

Nevada

Funway Holidays (081-466 0222)
Las Vegas: seven nights at the Golden Nugget Hotel costs from £489 to £629 per person, flight inclusive.

New England

Bon Voyage (0703 330332)
A 15-day self-drive tour of New England taking in Boston, Portland, Bar Harbour, White Mountains, Killington, Springfield, Newport and Cape Cod costs from £275 to £365 per person, based on two adults sharing a room with up to two children under 12 years accommodated free. This price does not include airfares.

New England Country Homes (0328 856666)
Hotels, country inns, small bed and breakfasts and working farms are offered by this booking service. An administrative charge of between £75 and £100 per holiday is made depending on the amount of time spent in planning the trip. Payment for the accommodation is paid to the individual properties at the end of the stay.

Virgin Holidays (0293 617181)
Destinations include Boston, Cape Cod, Kennebunkport, Rutland and Mystic. Two-centre holidays are offered in which you can combine any two New England states or a week in New England with a week in Florida. A seven-night stay at the Yankee Clipper Inn in Rockport, Massachusetts costs from £459 to £619 per person, including flights.

Virginia

Bon Voyage (0703 330332)
A three-centre self-drive tour to Washington, Williamsburg and Wintergreen. Prices range from £396 to £464 per person, based on two adults sharing a room with up to two children under 12 years accommodated free. These prices do not include airfares.

United States: in more than one state

America Ad Lib (0732 867300)
American Dream offers a range of hotels throughout the USA, from budget to luxury. Prices range from £535 per person in the low season to £1925 per person at Christmas.

American Independence (0371 874848)
Hotel inclusive deals to Florida and other parts of the States: a seven-night package to San Francisco, for example, costs from £580 to £830 per person including return air travel.

Jetsave (0342 312033)
Hotel-inclusive packages to the US, mainly to Florida.

Jetset Tours (061-953 0920)
Hotel-inclusive packages to many destinations in the States, especially Florida. Seven-night packages to Orlando, for example, cost from £399 including return air travel.

BED AND BREAKFAST IN AMERICA

For travellers familiar with the British concept of bed and breakfast, the dismal picture this conjures up is one of lino floors, brinylon sheets, damp cupboards and severe landladies who have never cared to develop their inter-personal skills. In America, however, bed and breakfast is quite a different proposition.

It's largely an up-market concept. Prices for bed and breakfast accommodation in the States are usually not cheap – motels cost less – but value for money is generally outstandingly good. The houses are usually furnished to a very high standard; hosts and hostesses are normally very welcoming and hospitable.

An indication of how many bed and breakfast places there are in the States is given by the fact that there are more than 150 reservation organizations throughout the States. The reservation offices, which normally cover a small geographical region, are very efficient. Home Base Holidays (081-886 8752) publishes an annually up-dated guide *Bed and Breakfast in the United States and Canada* (price £4.25 including postage and packing) which lists bed and breakfast reservation agencies and host homes.

Other useful guides include *Frommer's Bed and Breakfast North America* (Frommer Books, $14.95) which provides a comprehensive list of reservation agencies and a selection of the 100 best bed and breakfast homes in North America and a directory of more than 200 bed and breakfast inns; *Bed and Breakfast Inns & Guest Houses in the United States and Canada* (John Muir Publications, $15.95) listing more than 5,500 inns; *Treasury of Bed and Breakfast – North America* (American Bed and Breakfast Association, 10800 Midlothian Turnpike, Suite 254, Richmond, VA 23235-4700, Tel: 804-379 2222, $14.95); *The Official Bed and Breakfast Guide for the US, Canada and the Caribbean* (PO Box 332, Norwalk, CT 06852, Tel: 203-847 6196, $19.95).

Main US Bed and Breakfast Agencies

Northwest US: Northwest Bed and Breakfast Travel Unlimited, 610 SW Broadway, Suite 606, Portland, OR 97205 (503-243 7616).
Western US: Bed and Breakfast Rocky Mountain, 673 Grant Street, Denver CO 80203 (800-733 8415); Bed and Breakfast International, PO Box 282910, San Francisco, CA 94128-2910 (415-525 4569).
Eastern US: Pineapple Hospitality, PO Box 7821, New Bedford, MA 02742 (508-990 1696); American Country Collection of Bed & Breakfasts, 4 Greenwood Lane, Delmar, NY 12054 (518-439 7001).
National US: Bed and Breakfast National Network, PO Box 4616, Springfield, MA 01101.

State bed and breakfast booking services

Alaska: Stay with a Friend Bed & Breakfast Reservations, 3605 Arctic Boulevard, Suite 173, Anchorage, AK 99503 (907-278 8800); Accommodations in Alaska, PO Box 110624-TA, Anchorage, AK 99516 (907-345 4761); Alaska Private Lodgings, PO Box 200047-F, Anchorage, AK 99520-0047 (907-258 1717); Alaska Sourdough Bed and Breakfast, 889-TA Cardigan Circle, Anchorage, AK 99503 (907-563 6244).
Arizona: Bed and Breakfast in Arizona, PO Box 8628, Scottsdale, AZ 85252 (602-995 2831); Arizona Association of Bed & Breakfast Inns (602-231 6777); Mi Casa Su Casa (800-456 0682).
Arkansas: B and B of the Arkansas Ozarks, Route 1, Box 38, Calico Rock, AR 72519 (501-297 8764); Arkansas Ozarks B&B, HC61 Box 72, Calico Rock, AR 72519.
California: Bed & Breakfast International, PO Box 282910, San Francisco, CA 94128-2910 (415-696 1690).
Colorado: Bed & Breakfast Rocky Mountains, 673 Grant Street, Denver CO 80203 (303-860 8415).

Connecticut: Nutmeg Bed & Breakfast, PO Box 1117, West Hartford, CT 06127-1117 (203-236 6698).
Delaware: Bed & Breakfast of Delaware, PO Box 177, 3650 Silverside Road, Wilmington, DE 19180 (302-479 9500).
District of Columbia: Bed & Breakfast Accommodations Ltd, PO Box 12011, Washington, DC 20005 (202-332 3510).
Florida: Bed & Breakfast Co, Tropical Florida, PO Box 262, Miami FL 33243-0262 (305-661 3270).
Georgia: Atlanta Hospitality, 2472 Lauderdale Drive NE, Atlanta GA 30345 (404-493 1930); Bed & Breakfast Atlanta, 1801 Piedmont Avenue NE, Suite 208, Atlanta, GA 30324 (404-875 0525).
Hawaii: Bed and Breakfast Hawaii, PO Box 449, Kapaa, HI 96746 (808-822 7771).
Idaho: Bed & Breakfast Idaho, PO Box 7323, Boise, ID 83707 (208-336 5174).
Illinois: Bed & Breakfast/Chicago, PO Box 14088, Chicago IL 60614-0088 (312-951 0085).
Iowa: Iowa Bed & Breakfast Innkeepers Association, PO Box 249, Avoca, IA 51521.
Kansas: Kansas Bed and Breakfast, Route 1, PO Box 93, WaKeeney, KS 67672 (913-888 3636).
Kentucky: Bluegrass Bed & Breakfast, Route 1 PO Box 263, Versailles, KY 40383 (606-873 3208).
Louisiana: Southern Comfort B&B Reservation Service, PO Box 13294, New Orleans, LA 70185-3294 (504-861 0082).
Maine: Bed & Breakfast Down East Ltd, PO Box 547, Eastbrook, ME 04634-9744 (207-565 3515).
Maryland: Bed & Breakfast of Maryland, PO Box 2277, Annapolis, MD 21404-2277 (410-269 6232).
Massachusetts: Bed & Breakfast Associates Bay Colony, PO Box 57166 Babson Park, Boston, MA 02157-0165 (617-449 5302).
Michigan: Lake to Lake Bed and Breakfast, Route 2, PO Box 183, Cedar, MI 49621 (800-832 6657).
Minnesota: Michel Farm Vacations, 45 Main Avenue N, Route 1, PO Box 914), Harmony, MN 55939 (507-886 5392).
Mississippi: Lincoln Ltd Bed and Breakfast, PO Box 3479, Meridian, MS 39303 (800-633 6477).
Missouri: Ozark Mountains Country Bed & Breakfast Service, PO Box 295, Branson MO 65616 (800-695 1546); Kansas City Bed & Breakfast, PO Box 14781, Lenexa, KS 66215 (913-888 3636).
Montana: Bed and Breakfast Western Adventure, PO Box 20972, Billings MT 59104 (406-259 7993).
New Jersey: B&B Adventures, Bay Street, Suite 132, Westport, CT 06880 (800-992 2632).
New Mexico: Bed & Breakfast Rocky Mountains, 673 Grant Street, Denver CO 80203 (303-860 8415).

New York: New York State: Bed & Breakfast USA, PO Box 606, Croton-on-Hudson, NY 10520 (914-271 6228); North Country B&B Reservation Service, PO Box 286, Lake Placid, NY 12946 (518-523 3739); Central New York Hospitality, PO Box 99, Edmeston, NY 13335 (607-965 8076); New World Bed & Breakfast, 150 Fifth Avenue, Suite 711, New York, NY 10011 (212-675 6366).

North Carolina: North Carolina Bed and Breakfast Association, PO Box 1077, Asheville, NC 28802 (800-849 5392).

Ohio: Buckeye Bed & Breakfast, PO Box 130, Powell, OH 43065 (614-548 4555).

Oklahoma: Redbud Reservations, PO Box 23954, Oklahoma City, OK 73123 (405-720 0212).

Oregon: Gallucci Hosts Hostels, PO Box 1303, Lake Oswego, OR 97034 (503-636 6933); NW Bed and Breakfast Travel Unlimited, 610 SW Broadway, Suite 606, Portland, OR 97205 (503-243 7616); Oregon Bed & Breakfast Directory, 230 Red Spur Drive, Grants Pass, OR 97527 (503-476 2932).

Pennsylvania: Rest & Repast B&B Service, PO Box 126, Pine Grove Mills, PA 16868 (814-238 1484).

Rhode Island: Bed & Breakfast of Rhode Island, PO Box 3291, RI 02840 (401-849 1298).

South Carolina: Historic Charleston Bed and Breakfast, 43 Legare Street, Charleston SC 29401 (803-722 6606).

Tennessee: Bed & Breakfast Hospitality International, PO Box 110227, Nashville, TN 37222-0227 (615-331 5244); Bed & Breakfast in Memphis, PO Box 41621, Memphis, TN 38174 (901-726 5920).

Texas: Bed and Breakfast Texas Style, 4224 W Red Bird Lane, Dallas, TX 75237 (214-298 5433); Sand Dollar Hospitality Bed and Breakfast, 3605 Mendenhall, Corpus Christi, TX 78415 (512-853 1222).

Utah: Bed and Breakfast Inns of Utah, PO Box 3066, Park City, UT 84060 (801-645 8068).

Vermont: Vermont Country Inns and B&Bs, Vermont Chamber of Commerce, PO Box 37, Montpelier, VT 05601 (802-223 3443).

Virginia: Bensonhurst of Richmond, 2036 Monument Avenue, Richmond, VA 23220 (804-353 6900); Guesthouses, PO Box 5737, Charlottesville, VA 22905 (804-979 7264).

Washington State: Bed and Breakfast Service (BABS), PO Box 5025, Bellingham, WA 98227 (206-733 8642); Pacific Bed and Breakfast Agency, 701 NW 60th Street, Seattle, WA 98017 (206-784 0539).

Wisconsin: Wisconsin Bed and Breakfast Homes and Historic Inns Association, 1020 Oak Street, Wisconsin Rapids, WI 54494 (715-424 2001).

UK agency for US bed and breakfast bookings

Colby International, 139 Round Hey, Liverpool L28 1RG (051-220 5848) arranges bed and breakfast bookings in cities throughout the States with prices for a double room costing from around £30 per night bed and breakfast; the agency can also arrange accommodation in 'unhosted' apartments.

6

ACTIVITY & SPECIAL INTEREST HOLIDAYS

ADVENTURE HOLIDAYS

American Adventures (0892 511894)
Seven, 14, 21, 28 and 42 day camping tours throughout America. For example, a 14-day Alaska Wildlife Safari which explores Alaska, the Yukon and Denali National Park costs from £399 to £429 per person. This price does not include return air tickets. 'This is one of the most challenging North American trips. You will travel through wilderness areas, at many stops the facilities will be basic, and the nightlife what we make ourselves.' A 14-day Indian Lands tour, visiting Indian tribal lands, old cowboy towns, the Grand Canyon and remote Canyonlands costs from £399 to £499 per person, exclusive of airfare. Tours to Arizona, Utah and Colorado – Grand Canyon. National Park wilderness expeditions and river rafting. Riverside, beach camp accommodation. Escorted by professional boatmen and canyon experts. Three- to 14-day trips range from $535 (£357) to $1895 (£1263), not including the cost of air travel from the UK.

Contiki Travel (081-290 6422)
Tours by coach for young people. Trips last from 3 to 47 days and include most areas of America. For example, a Northern Contrasts tour which starts in Chicago and ends in Santa Barbara lasts for 13 days and costs from £545 to £599 per person. This price includes accommodation, some meals and coach transport.

Explore Worldwide (0252 319448)
California, Yosemite and the Grand Canyon from June to September. Trips are for 21 days and include hotel accommodation and camping. Exploring the great outdoors of California's mountain and deserts by small maxi-wagons, plus a three-day hike across the Grand Canyon. The group size is from 6 to 12 people. Prices are from £1230 per person, flight inclusive. Thirty-one-day trips to the Yukon and Alaska from July to September cost from £1595 per person, including flights. The trip is overland from Vancouver to Anchorage by small maxi-wagons. The group size is between 6 and 12 people. Accommodation is in hotels and camping.

Ranch America (081-868 2910)
Ranch holidays in America from £710 per week, air inclusive. Cattle drives in Montana. An eight-day trip costs £1017 per person.
TrekAmerica (0869 38777)
Treks available throughout the USA. Over 40 different itineraries available, lasting from seven days to nine weeks. All tours are camping holidays with occasional hotel stops when visiting cities. Prices vary depending on length of trip and departure date. One week in Alaska in June would cost £289 excluding airfare and including all camping equipment, admission to all National Parks and monuments en route, a full day boat tour of Kenai Fjords National Park and the opportunity to go gold panning.
Virgin Holidays (0293 617181)
Railroad adventure holidays cost from £529 to £729 per person, including flights and train journeys.

ART & ARCHITECTURE TOURS

Specialtours (071-730 3138)
Escorted tours. For example, a nine-night tour to Philadelphia costs £1575 per person, flight inclusive.

BATTLEFIELD TOURS

Major and Mrs Holt's Battlefield Tours (0304 612248)
American Civil War: a trip covering the Mississippi Campaign costs £1585 per person, including flights, coaches, hotels, guides, all entrances and breakfast.

CITY BREAKS

American Dream (081-470 1181)
One-, three- and seven-night stays in Boston, Washington, New York and New Orleans. A three-night break at the Omni Park Central Hotel in New York costs from £234 per person, exclusive of airfare.
Bon Voyage (0703 330332)
Breaks in all the major American cities. Prices range from £30 in San Diego to £165 in New York and are per room, per night.
British Airways Holidays (0293 617000)
New York, Boston and Washington. For example, a seven-night stay in Washington at the Barcelo Washington Hotel, 'just one and

a half blocks from the White House' costs from £569 to £916 per person, based on two sharing, flight inclusive.

Donald Mackenzie (041-221 5539)
Destinations include Boston, Chicago, Washington and New York. For example, a three-night break to Chicago costs from £522 to £648 per person, air inclusive.

Flightbookers (071-757 2000)
New York: a seven-night stay at the Milford Plaza costs from £499 to £643 per person. This price includes accommodation, flights and car hire.

Frontiers Travel (081-742 1488)
All the popular destinations in North America, including Hawaii. A three-night trip to New Orleans, for example, costs from £141 per person, based on two sharing a room. Flights are not included.

Funway Holidays (081-466 0222)
Short breaks to Las Vegas, New York and Orlando. For example, two nights in Las Vegas staying at the Hacienda Hotel and flying from London, Manchester or Glasgow with American Airlines costs from £359 per person, with car rental from £20 per day.

Getaway (081-313 0550)
Weekends to Boston or New York start at £299 per person for a two-night stay, flight inclusive.

Jetset Tours (061 953 0920)
Weekend breaks to New York, Boston and Washington. A three-night holiday in Boston, for example, costs from £377 to £543 per person. The price includes return flights and three nights' accommodation.

Key to America (0784 248777)
Weekend breaks to New York, Boston and Washington. For example, a three-night stay at The Dorset Hotel, situated in Central Manhattan costs from £345 to £525 per person, flight inclusive.

Northwest Airlines (0424 732777)
Three-night stays in cities across America. For example, a stay in Atlanta costs from £66 to £141 per person, based on two sharing. Airfares are not included.

Osprey Holidays (031 557 1555)
Two-, four- and five-star hotels in central New York. A two-night room-only break at the two star Murray Hill Hotel costs from £299 to £484 per person, including air travel from London. Two nights at the five-star InterContinental costs from £399 to £569 per person.

Page & Moy (0533 524433)
Four- or five-night breaks to New York from Heathrow, Manchester, Birmingham or Glasgow. Prices range from £329 to

£369 per person for the four-night tour. This price includes air travel and accommodation at a central hotel but excludes meals.

Peltours (081-346 9144)
Seven-night breaks in New York cost from £569 to £1218 per person, flight inclusive.

Peregor Travel (0895 639900)
New York and Boston. For example, a weekend in Boston, travelling with Virgin Atlantic costs from £255 to £433 per person, based on two sharing.

Thomas Cook (0733 68519)
Los Angeles, New Orleans, New York, Orlando, San Diego, San Francisco and Washington DC. For example, a four-night Los Angeles mini-break costs from £131 to £142 per person, with accommodation at the Holiday Inn Buena Park and entrance to Disneyland, Universal Studios and Knotts Berry Farm. This price does not include air fares.

Thomson Holidays (021-632 6282)
Boston, New York and Washington. For example, a three-night stay in Washington at the Latham, a colonial style hotel which is situated in Georgetown and has an outdoor pool costs from £359 to £549 per person, flight inclusive.

Time Off (071-235 8070)
New York and Boston. A weekend break to New York staying at a two-star hotel costs from £427 to £544 per person, flight inclusive.

Travelscene (081-427 4445)
New York and Boston. For example, a three-night stay in New York at the five-star Westbury Hotel, flying with either Virgin Atlantic or British Airways costs from £589 to £819 per person.

United Vacations (081-313 0999)
New York, Washington, Boston, Chicago, New Orleans, Denver, Seattle, Los Angeles and San Francisco. For example, a three-night stay at the Holiday Inn Crowne Plaza in Seattle costs from £412 to £578 per person, flight inclusive.

Virgin Holidays (0293 617181)
A three-night theatre break to New York costs from £379 to £509 per person, including return air travel, transfers and accommodation. New York 'Broadway Breaks': three nights' accommodation, return flights and tickets for a Broadway show costs from £384 to £538 per person. A 'Manhattan Shopping Break' which includes three nights' accommodation and return flights costs from £351 to £505 per person.

CLUB HOLIDAYS

Club Med (071-581 1161)
Situated in Port St Lucie, Florida, the Sandpiper village is located in 1,000 acres of gardens near two golf courses. A sandy beach is 20 minutes away by shuttle from the village. Accommodation is in twin-bedded air-conditioned rooms with bathroom, telephone, television and mini-fridge. These are set on three levels and either have a private terrace or balcony. It is also possible to add a child's bed. A 14-night holiday costs from £1501 to £2496 per person. This price includes flights, full board including wine with meals, most sports activities and entertainment.

COACH HOLIDAYS

American Connections (0494 473173)
An escorted coast to coast coach tour. The trip lasts for 21 days and visits New York, Philadelphia, Washington, Niagara Falls, Toronto, Detroit, Chicago, Sioux City, Deadwood, Cody, Yellowstone National Park, Salt Lake City, Grand Canyon National Park, Lake Mead, Las Vegas, Los Angeles, Carmel, Monterey and San Francisco. The price is £1125 per person, based on two sharing and includes accommodation, air-conditioned motor-coach and admissions to the Henry Ford Museum, Mount Rushmore, Buffalo Bill Historical Centre, 17-Mile Drive, plus five National Parks. The price does not include meals.

American Independence (0371 874848)
Nine day tours of the Rockies and Parks and 13 day tours of the South-west. For example, a nine-day all inclusive Rockies and Parks tour featuring Mesa Verde, Vail, Aspen, Colorado Springs and the Rocky Mountain National Park starts from £1395 per person. Also included in the price are trips on the narrow gauge Durango/Silverton railroad and Pikes Peak Cog Railway.

Appleyard Tours (0565 755158)
Touring holidays of California, Florida, New England, Arizona and the Mid west. A tour of California featuring Los Angeles, San Diego, Las Vegas, Yosemite, San Francisco, San Simeon and Santa Barbara costs £899 per person for 12 nights, flight inclusive.

Archers Tours (081-466 6745)
Seven escorted coach tours which include the Eastern USA and Niagara Falls, New England in the Fall, the East Coast, the Golden West and the Parks and Canyons Spectacular. For example, a 21-day coast to coast tour from New York to Los Angeles costs from £1235 to £1309 per person, flight inclusive.

British Airways Holidays (0293 617000)
Escorted tours around many locations in the USA. For example, a South to Florida Tour which visits New York, Washington, Williamsburg, Durham, Cherokee Indian Reservation, Nashville, Memphis, New Orleans, Tallahassee and Orlando costs from £1095 to £1209 per person, flight inclusive.

Classic Tours (071-613 4441)
Escorted tours to Alaska, Arizona, California, Hawaii, New England, New Orleans, New York, Texas, Washington and Yellowstone National Park. For example, an eight-day trip to Washington and Williamsburg costs $869 per person, based on two sharing. This price does not include airfares.

Cosmos Coach Tours (081-464 3477)
A range of over 20 tours. For example, the 14-night Southern Trails and Virginia Beach tour which visits Washington DC, the Blue Ridge Mountains, Lexington, Nashville, Memphis, Gatlinburg, the Smoky Mountains, Asheville, Raleigh and Virginia Beach costs from £949 to £1049 per person, flight and accommodation inclusive.

Donald Mackenzie (041-221 5539)
Escorted tours to New England, Dixieland, the West Coast and Pennsylvania. For example, a Western Discovery Tour with flights from Glasgow via Chicago and visiting Los Angeles, the Mojave Desert, Las Vegas, the Grand Canyon, Yosemite National Park and San Francisco costs £965 per person, flight inclusive.

Funway Holidays (081-466 0222)
Seven escorted coach tours. A 17-day Best of the Rockies trip, for example, costs from £1129 per person. This price includes scheduled flights, accommodation and sightseeing trips to Rapid City, Black Hills, Yellowstone, Helena, Glacier National Park and Salt Lake City.

Getaway (081-313 0550)
Two escorted tours which both visit all the principal attractions of New England, accompanied by a professional tour director. For example, the New England Experience 11-day tour includes admission to Salem Homes, the Cape Cod-Martha's Vineyard ferry, Plimouth Plantation and a New England lobster dinner and costs from £777 per person. This price includes flights and mainly first class accommodation.

Hermis Travel (071-731 3979)
Escorted coach tours to the National Parks, New Orleans and the Deep South, and the West Coast. For example, the 13-day National Parks tour which visits Scottsdale, the Grand Canyon, Montezuma Castle, Bryce, Zion, Yellowstone, Grand Teton National Parks, Salt Lake City, Old Faithful and Mount Rushmore costs from around £1217 to £1395 per person, based on two

sharing. This price includes return flights, 12 breakfasts and 10 dinners. Pre- and post-tour hotels can be booked in advance. There is a no smoking policy on all coaches.

Jetsave (0342 312033)

Eleven escorted coach tours all over America. For example, the 16-day Southern Experience Tour visiting Dallas, San Antonio, Bandera, Corpus Christi, Houston, Galveston Island, New Orleans and Natchez costs from £909 per person to £1039, flight inclusive.

Jetset Tours (061-953 0920)

Over 40 coach tours throughout the USA. For example, a 14-day Golden West tour which visits Los Angeles, San Diego, Scottsdale, Rawhide, Williams, Grand Canyon, Hoover Dam, Yosemite National Park, San Francisco, Sausalito, Monterey, Carmel, San Simeon and Solvang costs £603 per person, based on two people sharing.

Key to America (0784 248777)

Escorted coach tours. For example, the 15-night West Coaster tour which includes Los Angeles, San Diego, Ensenada, San Felipe, Scottsdale, Grand Canyon, Las Vegas, Yosemite National Park, San Francisco and San Simeon costs from £1032 to £1199 per person, flight inclusive.

Kuoni Travel (0306 742222)

Ten escorted coach tours in various parts of America. The Grand New England tour, for instance, which visits Boston, Kennebunkport, White Mountains, Woodstock, Green Mountains, Newport, Cape Cod and Martha's Vineyard costs from £749 to £902 per person for nine nights, flight and accommodation inclusive.

N.A.R.(UK) Ltd (0753 855031)

Escorted coach tours. Popular itineraries with many departure dates. For example a seven-day Autumn in New England tour costs $1195 (£800) per person, not including airfares from the UK.

Northwest Airlines (0424 732777)

The Grand New England Tour visiting Boston, Portland, White Mountains, Killington, Green Mountains, Cape Cod and Martha's Vineyard costs from £833 to £963 per person, based on two sharing. This price includes flights, eight nights' accommodation on a room only basis, touring by coach, a final night traditional New England lobsterbake and various admission fees.

Page & Moy (0533 524433)

Tours to the Golden West, Dixieland and Florida, the Deep South, the Eastern States and New England. The Southern Charm tour which takes in Atlanta, Birmingham, New Orleans, Lafayette, Natchez, Montgomery and Savannah costs from £795 to £925 per person. This price includes scheduled flights, all coaching, 13 nights' accommodation, excluding meals, sightseeing and excursions including a cruise on a Mississippi paddle steamer and the services of a tour guide.

Peregor Travel (0895 639900)

Tours in California, the East Coast and the area around the Rockies. For example, the Eastern Classics tour which lasts for seven nights and visits New York, Niagara Falls, Corning and Washington costs £355 per person, excluding airfare.

Thomas Cook (0733 68519)

Among the tours available are Heritage of America; New Orleans, Deep South; National Parks; New England; Florida; Eastern Triangle; Western Highlights and Grand Western Highlights. For example, a nine-day Heritage of America tour which visits New York, Philadelphia, Amish Country, Gettysburg, Shenandoah Valley, Williamsburg and Washington DC costs £669 per person. This price includes accommodation and coach travel.

Thomson Holidays (021-632 6282)

Tours of California and the West, Florida and the South and New York and the East. For example, a West Coast Highlights, 15-day tour which visits Los Angeles, Monterey, San Francisco, Mammoth Lakes, Las Vegas, Anaheim, San Diego and Tijuana costs from £949 to £1115 per person, flight inclusive.

Transolar Travel (051-630 3737)

A three-week touring holiday in the Western USA, visiting the Grand Canyon, Monument Valley, Lake Powell, Rainbow Bridge, the Sierra Nevada Mountains, Yosemite National Park, Phoenix, Las Vegas, San Francisco, Los Angeles, San Diego and Tijuana. Prices range from £1189 to £1469 per person, including flights, coach travel and accommodation. Extras on the trip include a sightseeing flight by helicopter into the Grand Canyon, a city tour of San Francisco, a half-day raft excursion on the Colorado River, a night out in the Wild West town of Rawhide to see a Wild West gunfight and admission tickets to Disneyland, Universal Studios and Sea World of San Diego.

Travel 4 (071-281 6564)

Tours which can be dovetailed into tailor-made itineraries or taken in their own right. Departures are from Los Angeles, Orlando and New York. For example, the Eastern Seabreeze tour leaves from Orlando and lasts seven days, visiting Georgia, South Carolina, Washington DC and New York and costs around £389 per person. This price includes six nights' accommodation but does not include air travel.

Travelsphere (0858 410456)

Fully-escorted tours to the West Coast, Florida and New Orleans, the East Coast, New England, the National Parks, the South-west and Hawaii. For example, a 16-day tour of the South-west visiting Texas, New Mexico and Arizona costs from £845 to £945 per person. This price includes flights, accommodation, travel by coach and three train journeys.

Unijet Travel (0444 459191)
Thirteen- and 14-night coach tours to the East and West Coasts. For example, the California Adventure coach tour visits Los Angeles, Las Vegas, Mammoth Lakes, Yosemite National Park, San Francisco and Carmel. This costs from £799 to £955 per person, and includes flights and accommodation.

United Vacations (081-313 0999)
Tours on the East Coast and California. For example, a 15-day West Coast Fiesta tour costs from £903 to £1054 per person, flight inclusive.

Wallace Arnold Tours (0532 310739)
A Western Discovery Tour of 16 days which features California, Arizona, Nevada and Colorado costs from £939 to £1119 per person, inclusive of flights. A Sea to Shining Sea Tour which features California, Arizona, New Mexico, Texas, Louisiana, Mississippi, Tennessee, North Carolina, Virginia, Washington DC, Maryland, Philadelphia, New Jersey and New York costs from £1249 to £1419 per person, inclusive of flights and lasts for 23 days. 1993 prices.

CONCORDE HOLIDAYS

Goodwood Travel (0227 763336)
A one-way Concorde flight from London to New York, three nights at the Waldorf Astoria Hotel, a Manhattan city tour and a scheduled British Airways return flight costs £1995 per person.

CRUISES

American Connections (0494 473173)
Three- and four-night cruises operating out of Fort Lauderdale and visiting the eastern and western Caribbean and Bermuda. Prices start at £339 per person for a three-night cruise.

American Dream (081-470 1181)
Seven-night and eight-day Caribbean cruises out of Miami. An Economy cruise on the *SS Norway* costs from £582 to £883 per person, based on double occupancy. This cruise visits St Maarten in the Dutch Antilles, St Thomas and an island in the Bahamas before returning to Miami.

Bon Voyage (0703 330332)
Seven-day Caribbean cruises out of Miami calling at a private Bahamian island, Ocho Rios in Jamaica, the island of Grand

Cayman and Cozumel in Mexico, cost from £859 to £1099 per person in a Superior cabin. This price includes all meals and entertainment.

British Airways Holidays (0293 617000)
Three- and four-night cruises from Los Angeles to Mexico as additions to fly/drive itineraries. For example, a three-night cruise combined with an 11-night fly/drive trip costs from £599 per person.

Classic Tours (071-613 4441)
Two cruises: one a 16-day trip around Key West, the Florida Gulf Coast and the Mississippi Delta; the other a 10-day trip around the Colonial South on the Intracoastal Waterway. Prices on application.

Cunard (071-491 3930)
Inclusive American tours and holidays featuring the *QE2* and Concorde. For example, an eight-day Superliner Supersonic holiday costs from £1865 per person. This price includes a British Airways Concorde flight between London and New York, accommodation at the New York Helmsley Hotel or the Waldorf Astoria and a five-day voyage on the *QE2*. A New Englander inclusive American tour costs from £1275 for 13 days. This price includes five days of cruising on the *QE2*, hotel accommodation in New York, Boston, Portland, North Conway, Killington and Enfield, sightseeing tours and flights between Boston and London.

Hermis Travel (071-731 3979)
Three- and four-night cruises out of Port Canaveral and seven-night cruises from Miami. For example, a three-night trip on Premier Cruise Lines – the official cruise line of Walt Disney World – costs between £323 and £419 per person.

Jetsave (0342 312033)
Three-, four- and seven-night cruises to the Bahamas and the Caribbean which can be added on to a stay in Orlando. Prices for a three- and four-night cruise start at £745 per person. A seven-night cruise starts at £759 per person.

Key to America (0784 248777)
Cruises from Miami with Norwegian Cruise Line to the Caribbean. A seven-night itinerary on the *SS Norway* costs from £699 to £1149 per person, based on two sharing.

Norwegian Cruise Line (071-408 0046)
Cruises out of Miami and Los Angeles, coupled with hotel stays or fly/drive options. For example, a 14-night Dreamward holiday which includes six nights at the luxury resort of Bal Harbour in Florida plus a seven-day cruise in either the eastern or western Caribbean costs from £1274 to £2230 per person, depending on the season and type of cabin. This price includes flights and car rental while in Florida.

Princess Cruises (071-831 1881)

Destinations include Florida and the Caribbean, California and the Mexican Riviera, Alaska and New England. A 15-night cruise around Florida and the Caribbean with a stay in Orlando costs between £1100 and £2500 per person, depending on the season and the state-room grade booked. This price includes return flights, all accommodation, all meals and entertainment on board, port taxes and car hire in Florida. 1993 prices.

Royal Caribbean Cruise Line (0932 820230)

Destinations include the Caribbean – a year-round programme, the Bahamas, Bermuda, Alaska and California. Cruises range from three to twelve nights with an optional Cruise Plus programme of hotel stays at competitive rates. Cruises can also be added to a holiday already planned. The company offers free regional connecting flights to London from 16 UK airports. The 1994 price for a nine-day Caribbean fly/cruise is £945 per person.

Thomas Cook (0733 68519)

Florida and the Caribbean. For example, seven nights in Key Largo combined with seven nights cruising the Western Caribbean costs from £1099 to £1899 per person, based on two sharing.

Transamerica (0293 774441)

Three- and four-day mini cruises to the Bahamas from Port Canaveral or Miami, or seven-day cruises to the Caribbean from Miami. Transamerica offer two cruise lines sailing from Orlando's closest port, Port Canaveral – Premier Cruise Lines who are the official Walt Disney cruise company – so you can sail with all the Disney characters, including Captain Hook; or Carnival Cruise Lines which claims to be the world's largest cruise company. Seven- day cruises out of Miami are with Norwegian Cruise Line. A three-night Premier cruise costs from £273 to £325 per person, based on two sharing. A seven-night Norwegian Line cruise to St Maarten, St John and St Thomas costs from £689 to £945 per person.

CYCLING HOLIDAYS

In the land where the mountain bike was invented, it is perhaps not surprising that cycling holidays are experiencing a boom. Wherever you go, you see cars with bike racks transporting the latest model mountain bikes and one presumes that these are being carried with serious intent rather than just for show.

America is now very much a cycle-friendly country with plenty of cycle trails from which to enjoy a huge variety of scenery. Of course it is relatively simple to take your own bike to the States:

airlines will normally carry your bike free of charge as long as you pack it properly (turn the handles sideways and take off the pedals and anything else which sticks out – but check all this with your airline first). Travel bookshops in America are full of books and guides specially written for cyclists.

However you might prefer to travel as part of a group with a guide to show you the way, and perhaps with support vehicles to transport your luggage. Several companies specialize in bike tours (prices shown exclude cost of travel to the US):

American Youth Hostels, PO Box 37613, Washington DC 20013-7613 (202-783 6161): A variety of tours across America. Cyclists bring their own bikes and carry their own luggage. For example, a 10-day tour of Amish Country in Lancaster County, Pennsylvania costs £300; a 23-day tour along the California coast starting in San Francisco and ending in San Diego costs £580.

Backroads (UK booking: 071-433 3413): 'A mix of singles, couples, families and friends, our guests tend to be between 23 and 55 years of age. In 1992 our average group size was 19. On most trips, the distance between each night's lodging can be comfortably biked in three to five hours. We furnish detailed directions and maps for you to take on the road. Our support van is never very far away, and with Backroads you ride only as far as you want.' For example, a five-day camping trip to the wine country of Northern California costs $648 (£432), with an extra $50 (£33) for van transfer and $109 (£73) for bike rental.

Bicycle Adventures, PO Box 7875, Olympia, Washington, 98507 (800-443 6060): Specializes in the Pacific North-west, trips varying in length from three to eight days. For example, a six-day wine-tasting tour of the Napa and Sonoma Valleys costs £790.

Bikecentennial, PO Box 8308, Missoula, Montana, 59807 (406-721 1776): Transcontinental bicycle tours for cyclists 'with more experience', some two to three months long. A 10-day 600-mile trip from Glacier National Park to Yellowstone National Park in Montana costs £300; travellers must bring their own bikes and camping equipment.

Brooks Country Cycling and Hiking Tours, 140 West 83rd Street, New York, NY 10024 (212-874 5151): A range of tours from day trips to seven-day trips, mostly in the north-east of America. A four-day trip to Shelter Island (off Long Island) costs £330 including half-board accommodation.

Butterfield & Robinson, 70 Bond Street, Toronto, Ontario M5B 1X3, Canada (800-678 1147): Tours include a seven-day mountain bike tour of Taso, Chimayo and Santa Fe in New Mexico for £1256 including accommodation, meals and bike hire.

Classic Adventures, PO Box 153, Hamlin, NY 14464-0153 (800-777

8090): A six-day tour of Virginia's horse and hunt country, for example, costs £486.

Outward Bound USA, 384 Field Point Road, Greenwich, Connecticut 06830 (800-243 8520): Nine-day biking and camping tours of rural New England organised by the Hurricane Island Outward Bound School (participants are also taught how to maintain and repair their bicycles). Tours cost from £596 including camping equipment and meals (which tour members prepare themselves).

REI Adventure Travel, PO Box 1938, Sumner, Washington 98390-0800 (800-622 2236): A seven-day tour of the Monongahela National Forest in West Virginia costs £463 including bed and breakfast at lodges and cabins. A seven-day tour of Death Valley in California costs £433.

Vermont Bicycle Touring, Box 711, Bristol, Vermont 05443 (802-453 4811): Runs bike tours in Virginia, Pennsylvania, Cape Cod, Maine and Nova Scotia in addition to Vermont, varying in length from two to five days. Weekend tours of Vermont, for example, cost from £172 to £219 including accommodation in inns and small hotels.

FLY/DRIVE

America Ad Lib (0732 867300)

Destinations across America. For example, a one-week trip to New Orleans costs from £315 to £509 per person, based on two people sharing an economy car with unlimited mileage. Pre-paid hotel vouchers are featured from £29 per room, per night.

American Airlines (081-572 7878)

AA Holidays lets you mix and match any number of days, destinations and hotel stays in over 40 states. It also offers six pre-planned self-drive itineraries with hotel accommodation. Routes are planned with departures from Los Angeles, San Francisco, Seattle, Denver, Dallas/Fort Worth and Boston. For example, the 15-day Mountain Magic Explorer holiday which starts in Denver and visits Grand Lake, Moab, Monument Valley, Lake Powell, Bryce Canyon, Grand Canyon, Mesa Verde, Santa Fe and Salida costs from £640 to £653 per person, excluding air fare.

American Connections (0494 473173)

Flights by British Airways, Delta Air Lines, KLM, TWA and Northwest Airlines. Prices include return air travel and seven days' car hire including unlimited mileage based on a two-door economy car with Dollar Rent-A-Car. A seven-night fly/drive package with Delta Air Lines to Florida costs from £313 to £504 per person, for a party of four adults.

American Dream (081-470 1181)
Pre-planned or flexible holidays to New England, Cape Cod and the North-east, Tennessee and the West Coast. A New England and Cape Cod Special which is a 15-day pre-planned holiday beginning with two nights in Boston and visiting Kennebunkport, the White Mountains, Woodstock, Deerfield, Rhode Island, Cape Cod and Plymouth costs from £249 to £329 per person. This price does not include air fares.

American Independence (0371 874848)
Colorado: fly/drives start at £385 per person for seven nights. Fly/drive trails, which include pre-booked accommodation, and visit old frontier towns, original railroad routes, creeks and canyons start at £880 per person for 14 nights. A houseboat on Lake Powell is an optional add-on, and costs from £649 for seven nights.

British Airways Holidays (0293 617000)
Independent fly/drives with hotel vouchers and self-drive tours with pre-booked accommodation in many areas of America. For example, a seven-night independent fly/drive package to the southern states – arriving at either Atlanta, Dallas or Houston – costs from £313 to £688 per person. This price includes flights and car hire. Hotel vouchers are available from £32 to £42 per night. A 16-day Classic New England self-drive tour with pre-booked accommodation, detailed maps and information about attractions en route, costs from £665 to £938 per person.

C&B Holidays (0293 886006)
Suggested itineraries in different states in addition to the popular areas of Florida and California. For example, a seven-day trip to Georgia, flying to Atlanta, costs from £261 per person, flight and car rental inclusive. Pre-paid hotel vouchers are available from around £152 per person, per week, based on two sharing.

Donald Mackenzie (041-221 5539)
Flights are with Northwest, American, United and British Airways from Glasgow to Boston, Chicago, Washington or New York. Further destinations are then possible. Car rental is offered with Alamo Rent-a-Car Company and vehicles range in size from the American equivalent of a Vauxhall Nova to a Renault Espace. For example, a California fly/drive which includes air travel and one week's basic car hire ranges from £336 to £484 per person, based on four sharing. Pre-paid hotel vouchers are also available, and hotel rooms can be booked before you travel.

Falcon (061-745 7000)
Florida. Operated in conjunction with Dollar Rent-a-Car, prices include return flights to Orlando. A 14-night holiday costs from £259 to £529 per person, based on two sharing. Hotels can be pre-booked and there is also a hotel voucher scheme available.

Florida Vacations (0727 841568)
Return scheduled flights from major UK airports to all Florida airports and a car to suit your party size for one week. Car hire includes unlimited mileage and primary third party insurance. Collision damage waiver is not included. The price for one week's holiday ranges from £299 to £385 per person.

Frontiers Travel (081-742 1488)
Packages to Florida, the East Coast, Central USA, the West Coast and Hawaii. Prices range from £272 to £741 per person including flights, and one week's car hire with unlimited mileage.

Funway Holidays (081-466 0222)
Flights from Gatwick, Stansted, Manchester or Glasgow to over 200 cities, using only scheduled flights on American Airlines, United Airlines, US Air, Virgin Atlantic and British Airways. A return flight to Boston, for example, on Virgin Atlantic, costs from £239 to £429 per person. Car rental is arranged with the American company Alamo and the first week's car hire costs from £1, based on four adults sharing. A second week's car hire in Florida, for example, costs from £23 to £115, depending on the type of vehicle. Pre-paid hotel vouchers are also available from £15 per person, per night, based on two adults sharing. Pre-planned fly/drive holidays are offered, with a 14-day California Dreaming tour for example, costing £789 per person.

Getaway (081-313 0550)
Sixteen-day pre-planned fly/drives in New England. For example, the Classic New England itinerary takes the coastal route north from Boston to Bar Harbor, heads inland through New Hampshire for the White Mountains, Squam Lake and Killington, Vermont, then continues south to Springfield through the Berkshire Hills and on to Mystic seaport in Connecticut. Accommodation is pre-booked. Prices start at £697 per person.

Greaves Travel (071-487 5687)
The popular destinations in Florida and California plus Atlanta, Boston, Washington, Chicago, Detroit, Dallas, Houston, New York, Philadelphia, Pittsburgh, Denver, New Orleans and Seattle. A seven-day trip to Philadelphia, for example, costs from £279 to £499 per person. Hotel discount vouchers are available offering accommodation from £19 per family room, per night. Flights are with British Airways.

Hermis Travel (071-731 3979)
With Delta Air Lines to over 240 destinations. For example, a Frontier Land and Mountains fly/drive with destinations to Phoenix, Salt Lake City, Tucson, Albuquerque, Denver or El Paso costs around £356 per person for one week, based on two sharing. This price includes return flights and car hire. Your first night's accommodation can be arranged for you, and on most fly/drives

you can fly into one city and fly home from another. For those who want to plan their own fly/drive, but want the security of having it pre-booked with help to find the ideal route, Hermis has produced itineraries for the Far West and the South. You can plan your own route and then you will be sent a travel kit giving maps, tourist information and hotel vouchers specific to your individual tour.

Jetlife Holidays (0322 614801)
Destinations all over America plus Western Explorer multi-centre tours which combine six cities – Los Angeles, Anaheim, San Francisco, San Diego, Las Vegas and Phoenix – with any length of stay (up to seven days) in each. A seven-night holiday starts at £499 per adult, £199 per child, inclusive of return flights from Gatwick, car hire and accommodation.

Jetset Tours (061 953 0920)
A wide range of destinations, including Atlanta, Boston, New York, Philadelphia, Washington, Miami, Orlando, Detroit, St Louis, New Orleans, Chicago, Minneapolis, Dallas, Los Angeles, Las Vegas, San Francisco, Denver, San Diego, Phoenix and Seattle. A seven-day holiday to Washington, for example, costs from £311 to £458 per person based on two people sharing. The price includes the rental of a compact car and collision damage waiver.

Key to America (0784 248777)
Destinations include Florida, New England, Virginia and the Western States. For example, a pre-planned, 14-night fly/drive holiday to New England, arriving at Boston and visiting Portland, Bar Harbor, White Mountains, Killington, Springfield, Newport and Hyannis costs from £635 to £789 per person, based on two sharing. This price includes flights, accommodation and car hire with unlimited mileage.

Kuoni Travel (0306 742222)
Pre-planned tours which include Route 66, Best of the West, Alaskan Splendour and Virginia Highlights. The Route 66 tour which visits Chicago, St Louis, Springfield, Tulsa, Oklahoma City, Amarillo, Tucumcari, Albuquerque, Santa Fe, Grand Canyon, Las Vegas, Los Angeles and Santa Monica costs from £998 to £1449 per person, based on two sharing. This price includes accommodation, car rental and flights.

Lotus Supertravel (071-962 9933)
Self-drive itineraries: for example, a 14-day trip on a circular route from Miami to Key West costs from £355 per person. This price includes flights and pre-booked hotels.

Northwest Airlines (0424 732777)
Scheduled flights from Gatwick and Glasgow serve a coast to coast US network of 200 cities through Boston or Minneapolis/St Paul. Open jaw tickets, allowing you to fly to one US city and

return from another, pre-paid hotel vouchers and fly/drive tours are all featured. For example a California Dreaming fly/drive tour, visiting Los Angeles, Santa Barbara, Morro Bay, Monterey, San Francisco, Lake Tahoe, Yosemite and Sequoia National Park costs from £855 to £1005 per person, based on two sharing. This price includes accommodation, flights and car rental.

Peregor Travel (0895 639900)

Pre-planned tours to many areas including Texas, California, Florida, Arizona, New England and New Orleans. For example, the seven-night Florida Magic tour which visits Orlando, Fort Myers, Sanibel, the Everglades, Key West and Miami costs from £435 per person. This price includes flights, accommodation based on two sharing and car rental.

Sunworld (0532 393020)

Return flights to Orlando plus Dollar car rental. You arrange your own accommodation. Prices range from £329 to £499 per person for 14 nights.

Thomas Cook (0733 68519)

Pre-planned self-drive tours in many locations. For example, an eight-day tour around New Orleans, visiting Bellingrath Gardens, *antebellum* mansions, Natchez, Cajun country and Lafayette costs from £339 to £368 per person. The price includes accommodation, full American breakfast at each hotel, farewell dinner on the last night and maps and sightseeing information.

Thomson Holidays (021-632 6282)

Destinations include Los Angeles, San Francisco, Orlando, New York, Washington, Boston, Seattle, Denver, Houston and Dallas. For example, a 14-night holiday to Dallas costs from £429 to £589 per person. You can pre-book your first night's accommodation at your city of arrival or pre-pay for accommodation vouchers that can be used at selected hotels. Self-drive tours are also offered. These trips are planned to feature all the main attractions en route with confirmed hotel bookings each night. For example, a Pueblos and Canyons tour of California and the West costs from £975 to £1059 per person, flight and accommodation inclusive.

Transamerica (0293 774441)

A range of fly/drive options to popular holiday destinations, based on daily flights by Continental Airlines from Gatwick to New York, Denver and Houston with connections to seven Florida cities and all major cities in California, plus 80 other US towns. In addition the company offers daily departures from Heathrow, Stansted, Manchester and Glasgow with British Airways, American, Virgin, Delta, Northwest, TWA and US Air. A one-week holiday to Boston or Washington DC costs from £339 per person, based on two sharing an Economy class car.

Transolar Travel (051-630 3737)

Florida, Western USA and America coast to coast. Accommodation vouchers and pre-planned itineraries are offered. For example, the fly/drive price using British Airways from Heathrow to Miami for one week costs from £353 to £653 per person. Hotel vouchers range from £30 per room, per night. A 23-day tour of America from coast to coast, with hotel passes and a rental car with unlimited mileage ranges from £931 to £1106 per person, based on two sharing. This price includes flights from London to Los Angeles with return from Miami to London.

Travel 4 (071-281 6564)

Working in partnership with KLM, Travel 4 is offering fares to 11 US cities with the opportunity to fly from one of 17 UK airports. Flights are via KLM's international base at Amsterdam's Schiphol Airport. Baggage is checked through from the UK to the final destination. Car hire is with Dollar Rent-a-Car. For example, flights to Washington DC range from £279 to £403 per person. Car rental locations are situated throughout the USA and a compact car costs from £86 to £155 per week. This price includes unlimited mileage, CDW and liability insurance. Hotel passes offering over 1,200 properties in the Howard Johnson and Discover America hotel chains are also featured at between £30 and £95 per room, per night.

Travelscene (081-427 4445)

A seven-day New England Discovery holiday, using Sandwich as a base which is just an hour's drive from Boston, costs from £664 to £999 per person. This includes flights, accommodation at a four-star 18th-century style inn and car hire.

Ultimate Holidays (0279 755527)

Florida. Prices start at £279 per person for a seven-night holiday, based on four people sharing a compact car. This price includes your first night's accommodation at a four-star hotel, car hire with unlimited mileage and flights. A hotel voucher scheme, from £33 per night, is offered.

Unijet Travel (0444 459191)

Flights from Gatwick, Manchester, Birmingham, Glasgow, Stansted and Heathrow to many destinations across America. Open jaw flights and one-way car rentals are offered as an option. A fly/drive holiday to Boston, for example, costs from £275 to £449 per person. This price includes flights and car rental. Florida Selection and Western Selection holidays offer pre-planned routes with hotels paid for in advance. Hotel voucher schemes are also available.

United Vacations (081-313 0999)

United Airlines flies from the UK to the gateway airports of New York, Washington DC, Los Angeles, San Francisco and Seattle.

Prices to New York, including one week's car rental and one free stop-over range from £269 to £435 per person, based on two adults travelling together. Hotel vouchers are available from £28 per night.

GOLFING HOLIDAYS

Classic Tours (071-613 4441)
Golf holidays in the Carolinas. For example, a seven-day package at Harbour Town Villas which includes accommodation, seven rounds of golf and a budget mid-size car with unlimited mileage costs £517 per person, based on four golfers sharing a two-bedroom, two-bathroom villa. Flights are not included.

Golf USA (081-868 2910)
South Carolina, Arizona, California and Colorado. A week's holiday in Arizona costs from £1628 to £1787 per person. This includes flights, bed and breakfast accommodation, Hertz car hire and five rounds of golf.

Longshot Golf Holidays (0730 268621)
Myrtle Beach, Carolina: a seven-night bed and breakfast package costs from £499 per person. This price includes free golf, car hire and flights.

Lotus Supertravel (071-962 9933)
Florida: seven nights at the PGA course, Grenelefe with accommodation, flights, car hire and course fees starts at £299 per person.

North American Vacations (091 483 6226)
Destinations include Hawaii, Arizona, California, Georgia and Florida. For example a five-day holiday in Fort Myers, Florida costs from $369 to $479 per person. This price includes three days of golf. Air travel is not included.

Page & Moy (0533 524433)
Golfing packages to South Carolina. Prices from £799 for 10 days, including golf and half-board.

Sovereign Golf (0293 599911)
Myrtle Beach, Pawleys Island and Brunswick County in Carolina and Orlando and Crystal River in Florida. For example, seven nights at Pawleys Plantation Golf and Country Club in Carolina with a Jack Nicklaus designed 18-hole golf course, costs from £499 to £769 per person, based on six people sharing a three-bedroom villa. Five rounds of golf are included in the package.

Travelpack (061-707 4404)
Self-catering and resort accommodation on Longboat Key, Crystal River, Clearwater, Stuart and Grenelefe. For instance, a stay at the Grenelefe Resort which has three golf courses, five swimming

pools, whirlpools and saunas, a marina and a tennis complex costs from £23 to £60 per night, based on two sharing. Pre-paid golf rates – 18 holes plus cart – costs from £25 to £53 per person. Advance tee times are available.

HONEYMOONS AND WEDDINGS

America Ad Lib (0732 867300)
Honeymoons in Hawaii from around £1000 to £2500 per person.
Thomson Holidays (021 632 6282)
Florida: weddings in Orlando can be arranged in conjunction with the four hotels featured by Thomson Worldwide in Orlando. If you stay in the Sheraton Inn Lakeside, the Gateway Inn and the Grosvenor Resort you can choose to marry in Cypress Gardens. The supplement payable per couple on top of the basic price is £459 for a wedding there. If you stay at Dixie Landings Resort you can marry in Walt Disney World. The supplement payable for a wedding there is £629 per couple.
Virgin Holidays (0293 617181)
'Virgin Weddings' in Miami, Orlando, St Petersburg, Jamaica and St Lucia. In Miami, for example, for a flat charge the company will arrange a marriage licence, wedding ceremony at the hotel, flowers and a bottle of champagne: a photographer or video can be ordered. In Key Largo, divers can be married underwater (qualified divers only).

HORSE-RIDING

American Independence (0371 874848)
Dude ranch holidays in Texas: a seven-night package including two rides per day costs from £805 to £1045 per person including full-board and return air travel.
American Round-Up (0442 214621)
Riding tours of Arizona, California, Wyoming and Vermont. Seven-night vacations cost from £677 to £1070 per person, including full-board, either camping or hotel accommodation, all riding, baggage transportation from point to point and taxes. Air travel is not included.
Ranch America (081-868 2910)
Horseback trips in Arizona, Wyoming, Colorado and New Mexico. A six day trip ranges from £654 to £753 per person.

MOTOR RACING HOLIDAYS

Page & Moy (0533 524433)
Claims to be the largest organizer of travel to all Formula One
Grands Prix and a number of NASCAR championships in the
USA. Plus 'Be a racing driver for a day' from £180 per person.

MOTORCYCLING

Jetsave (0342 312033)
Harley Davidson Electra Glide Classic motorbike for hire in
Florida. All riders must be aged 21 or over and have held a full
UK motorcyclists licence for at least two years at the date of
rental. The rental per bike per day is £70. This price includes a
1993 model bike with 200 miles per day free mileage; insurance
including collision damage waiver, and wet gear for rider and
pillion; three large storage panniers per bike and one free full tank
of petrol. All bikes are fitted with AM/FM cassette stereo system.

MOTOR-HOMES

American Connections (0494 473173)
Pick-up points are in Denver, Los Angeles, Miami, New York,
Orlando and San Francisco. The daily price inclusive of CDW is
from £17 to £70. There is a peak season surcharge for all locations
except Miami and Orlando between 16 July and 15 August of £22
a day.
American Dream (081-470 1181)
Pick-up points are situated in Los Angeles, San Francisco, Denver,
Chicago, Miami and Las Vegas. Prices for an Intermediate vehicle
range from £44 to £102 per day. This includes 100 miles per day
and collision damage waiver insurance. Drivers must be aged 21
years and over.
American Independence (0371 874848)
Small, medium and large motor-homes in Colorado. Prices for a
medium motor-home range from £505 to £686 per person, for
seven nights. This price includes flights, a first night in a Denver
hotel, initial propane gas, basic collision damage waiver, camp-
ground guides and a starter kit.
Caravan Abroad (0737 842735)
Motor-homes ranging from 18-34 feet and sleeping from two
adults up to five adults or four adults and two children.
Suggested itineraries are shown in the brochure and some camp-
sites can be pre-booked before departure. The weekly rental for a

motor-home sleeping two adults and two children, with a pick up in Los Angeles costs from $399 (£266) to $819 (£546). This price includes 700 free miles.

Frontiers Travel (081-742 1488)

Rentals offered through the Cruise America or Go Vacations companies with centres across America. The minimum rental is for seven days. Prices range from £32 to £101 per day, for a vehicle sleeping two adults and two children.

Funway Holidays (081-466 0222)

Pick-up points across America. Motor-homes range in size from Mini which sleeps two adults to Large which sleeps two adults and four children. The price for a Large motor-home ranges from £60 to £105 per day. This price includes the first night's hotel accommodation, 100 miles per day and collision damage waiver.

Jetsave (0342 312033)

Major pick-up points in Los Angeles, San Francisco, Denver, Chicago and Miami. You may pick up and return to the same locations or take a one-way rental. Prices for an Intermediate motor-home are between £357 and £707 for one week. This sleeps up to five people. Included in the weekly rate is the first tank of propane gas; 100 miles a day; liability insurance coverage at statutory limits; collision damage waiver insurance; and your first night's hotel accommodation, based on four people per room occupancy. Drivers must be over 21 years of age.

Jetset Tours (061-953 0920)

A choice of six motor-homes, accommodating between two and six adults. Pick-up points throughout the USA. For example, a camper-van rented in Florida which sleeps four adults costs between £44 and £65 per day.

North American Vacations (091-483 6226)

Vehicles are available to rent from locations in Denver, Los Angeles, Miami, New York, Orlando and San Francisco. It is a condition of booking that all clients must have hotel accommodation for their first night in the USA. Prices range from $32 to $122 per day. One-way rentals are available on all vehicle types subject to an additional charge.

Thomas Cook (0733 68519)

Motor-homes, camper-homes and caravans. Rental locations include Atlanta, Chicago, Denver, Houston, Las Vegas, Los Angeles, Miami, Orlando, Phoenix, Salt Lake City, San Diego, San Francisco, Seattle and Tampa. Prices for a Standard motor-home which sleeps a family of five range from £43 to £99 per day. Minimum rental period is one week.

Thomson Holidays (021 632 6282)

Motor-homes are available from Los Angeles in California for 14- or 21-night holidays. Prices range from £439 to £739 per person for a motor-home that sleeps up to six people for 14 nights, flight inclusive.

Transamerica (0293 774441)
Over 15 pick-up locations nationwide. The camper price includes 100 miles daily, first tank of propane and return transfers from designated areas. For safety reasons clients are not allowed to pick up their camper on the day of their transatlantic arrival, so a hotel will need to be booked for their first night's accommodation. A C25 camper which sleeps five people and is 23-25 feet in length costs from £47 per day. The minimum rental period is seven days. For unlimited mileage add an additional £23 per day.

Music holidays

DB Jazz Tours (0789 267532)
Escorted holidays to the New Orleans Jazz Festival. Prices on request.

North American Vacations (091-483 6226)
Destinations include Memphis, Nashville and New Orleans. A four-night package to the Mardi Gras in New Orleans costs from $612 (£408) to $1005 (£670) per person, based on two sharing. This price does not include air fare.

Railway holidays

American Connections (0494 473173)
Rail tours with several itineraries, using the regular scheduled services of Amtrak. For example, The Desert Wind visits Denver, San Francisco, Los Angeles, Grand Canyon and Albuquerque and costs £756 per person. The price includes hotel accommodation and overnight train accommodation but does not include air fares.

Jetsave (0342 312033)
'A nostalgic journey on western railroads' featuring the Grand Canyon Railroad, Amtrak's South West Chief, the Cumbres and Toltec Railroad, the Durango and Silverton Narrow Gauge Railroad and Amtrak's Californian Zephyr. A 15-day fully-escorted tour costs from £1119 per person, flight inclusive.

North American Vacations (091-483 6226)
'Golden Spike Nostalgic Railway Adventures'. For example an eight-day itinerary from Los Angeles to Reno costs $2321 (£1547) per person, based on two sharing. This price includes hotel accommodation, transportation on the Golden Spike, all meals and sightseeing.

RANCH HOLIDAYS

American Independence (0371 874848)
Stays of one night or more can be arranged at dude ranches and frontier towns. Seven-night stays cost from £770 per person at the Strater Hotel in Durango or from £699 per person at the Skyline Ranch, Telluride.

American Round-Up (0442 214621)
Ranch holidays – ranging from working spreads to luxury resorts in Arizona, Colorado, Montana, Michigan, Texas, Wyoming and Utah. Seven-night vacations cost from £390 to £1079 per person, including full-board accommodation, all riding, ranch activities and taxes. Cattle drives and round-ups are offered in Montana, Wyoming and Utah. Seven nights on the range costs from £434 to £945 per person, including all meals, tents or tepees, all riding and taxes. Horse drives are featured in California. Two to five nights costs from £338 to £517 per person, including all meals, tents and riding. Air travel is not included in any of the prices.

British Airways Holidays (0293 617000)
Texas ranch holidays. 'Your chance to live the life of a Texas-style cowboy in the company of the Hicks family – at the Mayan Ranch, just 47 miles from San Antonio. Enjoy a packed hill-country programme of cook-outs, hiking, riding, square dances, entertainment, sports and more.' There is also a children's programme for 3 to 18 year olds. The price for an eight-night holiday costs from £970 to £1320 per person, based on two sharing, flight inclusive.

Jetsave (0342 312033)
Guest ranches in Arizona and Texas. Seven nights at the Mayan Dude Ranch in Texas costs between £805 and £959 per person, flight inclusive. A free Grade C Hertz car is provided with this holiday.

North America Travel Service (0532 432525)
Arizona, Texas and Wyoming. Two weeks on the Tanque Verde Ranch in Tucson, Arizona costs from £1934 to £2218 per person, including all activities, meals and return flights.

Northwest Airlines (0424 732777)
Three nights at the Tanque Verde Ranch in Arizona costs from £222 to £279 per person, based on two sharing. Air fares are not included. All meals, riding, use of all ranch facilities and transfers from/to Tucson Airport are included.

Ranch America (081-868 2910)
Working, dude and guest ranches in Texas, Arizona, New Mexico, Wyoming, Colorado and Montana. A seven-night stay at the Mayan Dude Ranch in Texas costs from £795 to £940 per person, flight inclusive. The price also includes full-board accommodation.

Thomas Cook (0733 68519)
Ranches in Arizona, Colorado, Texas and Wyoming. For example, a week on the Cherokee Park Ranch in Colorado costs from £636 to £653 per person, based on two sharing. The ranch features horseback riding and overnight trips, sightseeing trips in 4X4 vehicles, fishing, hiking and river rafting. 'All meals are served family style in the main lodge with plenty to satisfy most tastes. Cook-outs and barbecues are featured weekly.'

Virgin Holidays (0293 617181)
Ranch holidays in Arizona cost from £739 to £939 per person, including return air travel, full-board accommodation for seven nights and car hire.

RIVER BOATS

Jetsave (0342 312033)
Luxury river boats on Florida's St John's River, 45 minutes from Orlando. The boats are available on a seven-night rental basis and can be added on to a week's holiday in Orlando. The price for one week's rental is £875 for boats sleeping up to 10 people. Flights are not included.

RIVER RUNNING AND RAFTING

American Round-Up (0442 214621)
River rafting on the Snake River, Green River and the Colorado River. Expeditions last from two to five nights and cost from £238 to £665 per person, including all meals, boats and equipment and a river guide. Air travel is not included.

North America Travel Service (0532 432525)
White water rafting offered in Utah, Arizona and Colorado. Prices on application.

North American Vacations (091-483 6226)
White-water rafting in Utah. A trip on the Colorado River through Cataract Canyon and Canyonlands National Park with 26 rapids costs $680 (£453) per person, excluding air fare from the UK.

Ranch America (081-868 2910)
White-water rafting on the Colorado River costs from £440 per person for three days to £910 per person for six days.

SENIOR CITIZEN

Saga Holidays (0800 300 500)
California and Florida. For example, 15 nights at the Ramada Inn in Palm Springs costs from £649 per person.

SINGLES

Solo's Holidays (081-202 0855)
A 12-day skiing holiday in Colorado which costs £1275 per person and a 15-day Music Magic tour visiting New Orleans, Memphis, Nashville and Gatlinburg, which costs £1549 per person.

SKIING

In the past five years, America has emerged as a major destination for British skiers. Its rise in prominence is partly a result of our holiday love affair with all things American – but there are also good sound practical reasons for thinking about a ski holiday in the States.

Unlike skiing in the European Alps which developed haphazardly, being built around existing farming villages. In America, ski resorts are for the most part purpose-built. The American resorts in the Rockies, those particularly favoured by British ski operators and their clients, are at a much higher altitude – Breckenridge in Colorado, for example, is at 2,925m (9,549ft) compared with Kitzbuhel in Austria at 760m. This means that these resorts are open for longer – the American resorts traditionally open on Thanksgiving Day, the last Thursday in November – and they can expect to enjoy much better snow conditions. The quality of the snow in the States has been particularly attractive to British skiers over the past few years, since snow conditions in Europe have frequently been extremely disappointing.

America ski resorts also have the benefits of typically slick American organization. Lift queues are well managed, pistes are methodically prepared and well marked. Information on local conditions is updated regularly and is widely available. Ski lifts are more plentiful: with plenty of gondolas and cable cars to get you to the tops of mountains quickly and in comfort. Resorts employ ski guides who will provide ski tours free of charge. The resort of Vail, for example, even has a system of trafffic lights at the top of ski lifts to steer you away from busy runs. Skiers in America are polite and generally better behaved than their European counterparts.

But while it has its undoubted advantages, America also has its drawbacks. As the resorts are largely purpose-built you will find little of the olde worlde charm that makes the Tyrol attractive. And, it has to be said, that an American ski holiday will inevitably be more expensive: a seven-night package to Colorado will cost from around £500 compared with the Alps where prices start at around £250.

Main Resorts

Aspen, Colorado (2,422m):
The most fashionable of all the American ski resorts: celebrities you may bump into on the piste include film stars Michael Douglas and Jack Nicholson. The fact that it boasts a Hard Rock Cafe indicates the sort of people who visit the place. An old silver-mining town, Aspen has an attractive Victorian town centre (complete with horse-drawn carriages). It is certainly not the place for a cheap holiday but it offers good skiing for all levels of skier with plenty of nursery slopes and cross-country skiing trails. Aspen is a four-hour drive or a one-hour flight from Denver.
Operator: Ski the American Dream (081-552 1201)

Beaver Creek, Colorado (2,470m):
A 20-minute drive from Vail, and two and a half hours by road from Denver, Beaver Creek is a brand new resort where work on its construction began less than 15 years ago. The resort, which calls itself 'the most luxurious and comfortable ski resort in America', achieved a celebrity of sorts when former President Gerald Ford set up home here. It attracts an affluent clientele who can afford its high prices and who enjoy Beaver Creek's skiing which is particularly good for intermediate skiers. There are also very good facilities for children including children's centres which can accommodate all ages up to 12.
Operator: Ski the American Dream (081-552 1201)

Breckenridge, Colorado (2,925m):
One of the first of the American resorts to benefit from the British invasion, and is now featured by more than a dozen British ski specialists. Less than two hours drive from Denver – mostly by freeway – Breckenridge is easy to reach. It offers good skiing for the beginners as well as providing plenty of challenging runs for the expert. This range of skiing, combined with a good choice of budget-priced accommodation, makes Breckenridge the perfect place for a family skiing holiday. For those who do not wish to ski, you can go snow-mobiling through the woods at night and there is a fine skating rink on a natural pond.
Operators: Activity Travel (081-541 5115); American Independence (0371 874848); Bladon Lines (081-785 3131); Crystal (081-399

5144); Enterprise (0293 560777); Inghams (081-785 7777); Lotus Supertravel (071-962 9933); Made to Measure (0243 533333); Neilson (0532 394555); Ski Equipe (061-440 0010); Ski the American Dream (081-552 1201); Ski Thomson (021-632 6282); Ski Val (071-371 4900); Skiworld (071-602 4826).

Copper Mountain, Colorado (2,926m):
A purpose-built ski resort in business since the early seventies. A good place for family ski holidays with easy access to the slopes – which offer plenty of scope for beginners and intermediate skiers – and good childcare facilities (including an arts and crafts centre).
Operators: American Independence (0371 874848); Club Med (081-313 9900); Inghams (081-785 7777); Lotus Supertravel (071-962 9933).

Jackson Hole, Wyoming (1,924m):
A 90-minute flight from Denver, is rated by the experts as not only one of the best resorts in America, but one of the best ski places in the world. This is a genuine Wild West town with some of the most difficult skiing available. The lack of good nursery slopes makes it unsuitable for the beginner but there are plenty of activities for non-skiers: skating, indoor tennis, sledging, ten-pin bowling and much more. For example, you can take a snow-mobile ride up to Yellowstone National Park (home of the Old Faithful geyser) or visit the Ralph Lauren factory store.
Operators: Activity Travel (081-541 5115); American Independence (0371 874848); Collineige (0276 24262); Crystal (081-399 5144); Enterprise (0293 560777); Inghams (081-785 7777); Lotus Supertravel (071-962 9933); Made to Measure (0243 533333); Neilson (0532 394555); Ski Bound (0273 696960); Ski Scott Dunn (081-767 0202); Ski the American Dream (081-552 1201); Ski Thomson (021-632 6282); Ski Val (071-371 4900); Skiworld (071-602 4826).

Killington, Vermont (319m):
The most popular ski resort in north-east America, situated 150 miles from Boston in the New England state of Vermont. It claims to have the longest ski season of any America resort (running from mid-October to early June) with an annual snowfall of around 25 feet. And to supplement the God-given variety, the resort also boasts the world's biggest snow-making operation with snow-cannon covering 40 miles of trails. It is a good choice for families with a separate beginners' learning area and family workshops. There are also plenty of reasonably-priced hotels and motels and cheap eating places.
Operators: American Independence (0371 874848); Ski the American Dream (081-552 1201); Ski Thomson (021-632 6282); Virgin Holidays (0293617181).

Mammoth Mountain, California (2,425m):
A six-hour drive from Los Angeles (a spectacular run north from LA past the Mojave desert and up into the Sierra Nevada mountains), Mammoth Mountain has a long season, from November to May. It usually has an excellent snow record. It offers good nursery and childcare facilities, including a day centre. The resort offers free skiing for children under seven. There are around 130 marked trails and 30 lifts with much of the skiing above the treeline. A visit to Mammoth provides a good combination for a two-centre holiday with a further week in Los Angeles.
Operators: American Independence (0371 874848); Ski the American Dream (081-552 1201); Virgin Holidays (0293617181).

Park City, Utah (2,104m):
Once a prosperous town made rich on the income from silver-mining. The resort has capitalized on its colourful past to create an ambience that cleverly combines a Wild West tradition with the best in modern skiing. Less than an hour's drive from Salt Lake City, Park City is quite different to its near neighbour Snowbird. It spreads out along its valley, providing a good range of intermediate skiing and fine, safe slopes for beginners. For non-skiers activities include swimming, sleigh riding, indoor tennis and ice fishing. Both accommodation and eating out are reasonably priced.
Operators: Activity Travel (081-541 5115); American Independence (0371 874848); Crystal (081-399 5144); Lotus Supertravel (071-962 9933); Made to Measure (0243 533333); Ski the American Dream (081-552 1201).

Snowbird, Utah (2,468m):
Snowbird and its neighbour Alta, 25 minutes' drive from Salt Lake City, provide good skiing for the more advanced skier with a good system of lifts, fast runs and a good record of snow. With an average snowfall of 42 feet, Utah can justifiably claim to offer 'The Greatest Snow on Earth' Facilities for children and learners could be better, and prices tend to be expensive.
Operators: Activity Travel (081-541 5115); American Independence (0371 874848); Crystal (081-399 5144); Made to Measure (0243 533333); Ski the American Dream (081-552 1201).

Steamboat, Colorado (2,104m):
The old town of Steamboat was a traditional Wild West ranching town; the new ski resort of Steamboat is an ultra-modern purpose-built development. First developed in the sixties, the ski resort has developed into an area covering 2,500 acres with over 20 lifts and 100 separate trails. Not so glitzy as Colorado's other famous resorts Aspen and Vail, Steamboat is a fine place for family holidays with plenty of childcare facilities, good children's ski schools and even a children's 'nite club'. Accommodation and

restaurants are reasonably priced, with a good choice of apres-ski entertainment. Non-skiers can try bungee-jumping, bob-sleighing, ice-fishing or swimming in the town's hot-springs pool. Steamboat is an hour's flight from Denver.
Operators: Activity Travel (081-541 5115); American Independence (0371 874848); Crystal (081-399 5144); Enterprise (0293 560777); Lotus Supertravel (071-962 9933); Ski the American Dream (081-552 1201); Ski Thomson (021-632 6282).

Telluride, Colorado (2,660m):
Telluride secured its place in history long before the ski holiday business was dreamt of. It was here that Butch Cassidy and his infamous Hole in the Wall gang staged their first ever bank robbery. Butch wouldn't recognize the place now: since the early seventies the place has been transformed by the construction of a new ski village. Plans are afoot to develop Telluride into the country's premier ski resort. There is good ski teaching for children and beginners, a good record of snow but best of all are the stunning views which look almost Himalayan.
Operators: Activity Travel (081-541 5115); American Independence (0371 874848); Lotus Supertravel (071-962 9933); Ski the American Dream (081-552 1201); Skiworld (071-602 4826).

Vail, Colorado (2,500m):
Two and a half hours' drive from Denver, Vail is often suggested as the first American ski resort that British holiday-makers should try. The skiing is good for all abilities; it is particularly good for children offering what is claimed to be the largest ski school in the world with over 700 instructors. Children are catered for with a variety of special nurseries and clubs. For example, 'Six and Up' for 6 to 12 year olds, offers 'all day on-mountain adventure with video taping and a fun ski race'. Vail is not cheap but it is certainly cheerful, Austrian-looking with an excellent choice of hotels and restaurants – with an unrivalled array of apres-ski nightlife. Non-skiers can indulge in a wide range of activities from skating to bob-sleighing and snow-shoeing.
Operators: Activity Travel (081-541 5115); American Independence (0371 874848); Bladon Lines (081-785 3131); Crystal (081-399 5144); Enterprise (0293 560777); Inghams (081-785 7777); Lotus Supertravel (071-962 9933); Made to Measure (0243 533333); Neilson (0532 394555); Ski Equipe (061-440 0010); Ski the American Dream (081-552 1201); Ski Thomson (021-632 6282); Ski Val (071-371 4900); Skiworld (071-602 4826).

Specialist UK ski operators include:

American Dream (081-470 1181)
Resorts are situated in Colorado, British Columbia, California,

Wyoming, Vermont and Utah. The brochure gives very detailed information on each resort – on ski school and mountain services, activities off the slopes, facilities for children and piste and lift maps. For early and late season holidays, all of the major resorts feature state-of-the-art snow-making technology. Seven nights at the Hotel Jerome in Aspen, Colorado costs from £759 to £1415 per person, air inclusive.

American Independence (0371 874848)

Destinations include Vail, Aspen, Breckenridge, Lake Tahoe, Killington, Stowe and Sun Valley. For example, a catered chalet in Vail costs from £525 per person for seven nights including breakfast and dinner. This price includes return flights. Fourteen nights at The Lodge Hotel in Vail costs from £1756 to £2886 per person, flight inclusive.

Club Med (071-581 1161)

Copper Mountain, Colorado. A seven-night holiday costs from £1223 to £1377 per person. This price includes flights, full-board including wine with meals, ski tuition, ski pass and entertainment. Clubs are offered for children over three. Ski school from the age of six. Accommodation is in a modern hotel close to the centre of Copper Mountain and the ski lifts.

Crystal Holidays (081-399 5144)

Destinations include Aspen, Beaver Creek, Breckenridge, Crested Butte, Jackson Hole, Keystone, Killington, Lake Tahoe, Park City, Snowbird, Snowmass, Steamboat and Vail. Prices start at £369 per person, for seven days at the Chalet Killington, on a bed and breakfast basis in Killington, Vermont, with direct, non-stop flights with Virgin Atlantic from Gatwick to Boston. Ten day holidays start at £395, 14 days from £449 per person.

Inghams Travel (081-780 2277)

Self-catering and hotel holidays in Colorado and Wyoming. For example, a seven-night holiday to Jackson Hole in Wyoming, staying at the Sojourner Inn, costs from £543 to £774 per person, flight inclusive. A standard ski and boot package for six days costs £70 per person. A six-day ski pass costs £152 per person. Ski hire costs £48 per person.

Lotus Supertravel (071-962 9933)

Self-catering and hotel accommodation in Vail, Beaver Creek, Aspen, Snowmass and Steamboat in Colorado. A seven-night bed and breakfast package to Steamboat, for example, costs from £499 per person, flight inclusive.

North America Travel Service (0532 432525)

Destinations available are Colorado, Vermont and California. Prices on application.

Ski Enterprise (061-831 7000)

Self-catering apartments and hotel packages. Destinations include

Jackson Hole, Aspen, Vail, Steamboat and Breckenridge. For example, a 14-night holiday staying in Steamboat in the three-star Yampa View Condominiums which are apartments sleeping up to six people, costs from £563 to £699 per person.

Virgin Holidays (0293 617181)
Destinations include California, Vermont and New Hampshire. A seven-night stay at the Indian Head Resort in New Hampshire costs from £399 to £519 per person, flight inclusive.

STEAMBOATS

Classic Tours (071-613 4441)
Three- and four-night steamboat cruises on the Mississippi, combined with land tours. For example, a three-night cruise from New Orleans together with a tour which visits Natchez, the DeSoto National Forest, Bellingrath Gardens and the French Quarter of New Orleans costs from $1625 to $1915 per person, based on two sharing. Flights are not included.

The Delta Queen Steamboat Co (091-483 6226)
Two- to twelve night cruises on the Mississippi, Ohio, Tennessee and Cumberland Rivers. For example, a five-night Old South trip, which takes you from New Orleans to Memphis costs from $1250 to $2910 per person, based on two sharing. The price includes steamboat passage, accommodation, on board meals and entertainment. The trip includes visits to *antebellum* mansions, plantations and historical sites on the way.

TAILOR-MADE

Infinity Tours (071-924 3822)
Itineraries offered according to interests and budget. For example, sports holidays, Civil War tours or white water rafting. Rates available on request.

Trailfinders Travel Centre (071-937 5400)
Tailor-made itinerary service. Choose your airline, hotel and tour -'everything from camping trips in the Canyons to coach tours in New England'.

THEATRE BREAKS

Keith Prowse (0800 881882)
Two-night New York packages include two nights' accommodation at a choice of hotels and one Broadway theatre ticket. Prices

range from £130 to £265 per person, based on two sharing and depending on the category of hotel. Sightseeing tours of New York are also offered.

WALKING AND TREKKING

Backroads (071-433 3413)
Destinations include California, Washington, Montana, Utah, Vermont and Hawaii. 'Our group size ranges from 14 to 20 and includes a balance of singles and couples. We stay at mountain lodges, country inns, historic hotels, spas, villas, manor houses, castles and seaside resorts. Our walking vacations are designed for fitness and fun, not to test your stamina. We provide a van which is available whenever you've had enough walking for one day and want a lift.' A six-day inn trip to North-eastern Vermont costs $1195 (£796) per person, with an extra $50 (£33) for van transfer.

Ramblers Holidays (0707 331133)
Walking holidays to Washington State, New England, Virginia, Hawaii, Arizona, Colorado and Canyonlands. A two-week programme in New England staying in hotels and lodges on a half-board basis costs £1265 per person, including scheduled air travel. Two weeks' high altitude walking in the Rockies including 16 days on a bed and breakfast basis in hotels, motels and lodges costs from £995 to £1097 per person, flight inclusive.

TrekAmerica (0869 38777)
Adventure camping and trekking holidays throughout the USA, Canada, Alaska and Mexico. Small group journeys from seven days to nine weeks start at £320 – land only. Coast to coast trips range from three weeks to six weeks and start at £490. More adventurous treks in Alaska, Mexico and the Rocky Mountains are one to six weeks in duration with three-week itineraries starting at £570.

7

HOLIDAY AMERICA

It might seem stating the obvious somewhat to point out that America is a Big Country. But it needs to be said because British travellers often tend to forget just how big it is. The country covers a total area of over 3.5m square miles (by comparison the UK has an area of 93,638 square miles – which means that America is over 38 times bigger than Britain). To travel by road, for example, from New York on the East Coast to Los Angeles on the West Coast involves a drive of 2,794 miles (about the equivalent of London to Istanbul).

The size of the country inevitably means huge differences in climate, an extraordinary variety of geographical features and, of course, a large change in time zones (America's westernmost state Hawaii is five hours behind New York).

Despite this huge array of attractions and contrasts, most British travellers – particularly families – rarely look beyond Florida or California or New York for their holiday destination. This is a mistake. Nearly all parts of America offer fertile ground for a good family holiday – and given the high efficiency of America's service industries, everywhere is easy and relatively inexpensive to visit. Thanks to a comprehensive network of good, fast roads (but watch the speed limit!) and a massive network of regional domestic air services, it is easy to see a lot of the country in a short time.

This is a selection of the best destinations for a family holiday in America:

THE NORTH-EAST

Boston and New England
The city of Boston – perhaps best known these days as the home of the *Cheers* bar from the TV series – is perhaps the most historic of all American cities and one of the best for a short break. For a crash course in the history of Boston (and of America) follow the city's Freedom Trail, a line of red bricks set in the pavement which leads visitors past the main sights. The trail begins at the

Visitor Information Center on Boston Common (open daily 8.30am to 5pm Tel: 617 267 6466).

Boston's must-see places include the Museum of Fine Arts, the Isabella Stewart Gardner Museum, Beacon Hill and, of course, Harvard University in Cambridge. Children will no doubt be keen to visit the Computer Museum with exhibits that tell the history of computers.

But perhaps Boston's greatest attraction is that it serves as the principal gateway for New England, the collective description for the region which includes Cape Cod and its islands, Maine, New Hampshire, Vermont, Rhode Island and Connecticut.

After Boston, the best known part of New England is Cape Cod, a tongue of land poking out into the Atlantic, offering about 70 miles of coastline. The Cape has attractive old villages like Sandwich, Chatham and Falmouth – and along the Cape Cod National Seashore there are about 30 miles of unspoilt dunes and beaches. At Provincetown you will find the 252 foot high Pilgrim Monument which commemorates the arrival on the *Mayflower* of the Pilgrim Fathers.

Two off-coast islands worth considering are Martha's Vineyard (where they filmed *Jaws* and where Ted Kennedy's presidential aspirations foundered in the waters of Chappaquiddick), is a 45-minute ferry ride from Woods Hole on the mainland. The old whaling base of Nantucket, two and a quarter hours by ferry from Hyannisport, has a handsomely-preserved, elegant old town full of cobbled streets and antique houses – there are also some excellent paved bicycle paths.

On the Massachusetts coast other towns worth a visit include Plymouth, where the Mayflower Pilgrims settled, New Bedford, another ex-whaling centre, and Salem, where the infamous witch-hunts were conducted in the 17th century.

In inland Massachusetts, along the border with New York State, lies the Berkshire Hills, famous for its woods and handsome Victorian country mansions. In Lenox every July and August the Boston Symphony Orchestra has its open-air summer concerts at Tanglewood. Two good museums to look out for are Old Sturbridge Village – half-way between Worcester and Springfield – which enterprisingly recreates a New England village of the 1830s. The Hancock Shaker Village near Pittsfield tells the story of the strict religious community which lived here from 1790 to 1960.

The main attraction of states like Vermont and New Hampshire is the mellow scenery and the remarkable charms of old-fashioned American rural life. The key time to visit New England is during September, October and November when the fall foliage turns the trees into a kaleidoscope of autumnal colours. This is a perfect time for cruising the picturesque villages of New England.

There is a plentiful supply of inns and bed and breakfast places – and there are plenty of less expensive motels (see chapter 5). This is also a good place to rent a house: there are several agencies offering a good selection (see chapter 5).

Niagara Falls and New York State

There's much more to New York State than New York City (see chapter 9). Consider, for example, the Hudson Valley and the Catskills (here you will find Woodstock, site of the famous 1969 festival and present home of Bob Dylan). In the Adirondacks is Saratoga Springs, Lake Placid which has twice hosted the Winter Olympics and Cooperstown, the home of baseball which has the National Baseball Hall of Fame. Little more than an hour's drive from central Manhattan, the rural communities and rich farmland of Long Island are a world away. It's worth taking time to explore the Hamptons: Southampton is a famous hang-out for the New York smart set. More charming is Sag Harbor, on the South Fork.

The state's best known tourist attraction is Niagara Falls which used to be the main destination for American honeymooners (Oscar Wilde acidly described the falls as 'the second major disappointment of American married life'). The Falls, which lie on the border between America and Canada, are not the highest or widest but with a flow of water of more than 700,000 gallons per second in the summer, they are certainly the wettest. The best way to see the Falls is to take the Maid of the Mist tour right to the base of the Falls.

Philadelphia and Pennsylvania Dutch Country

While its name may be Greek for 'the city of brotherly love', Philadelphia has recently earned a less salubrious reputation as a place with a serious crime problem. But tourists who by day stick to the busy downtown sightseeing areas, and by night take taxis, will see only a cheerful, historic city.

The city lays claim to 'the most historic square mile in America' with its Independence National Historical Park. The main sight here is Independence Hall where the Declaration of Independence was adopted on 4 July 1776. The Declaration of Independence was first read in public in nearby Independence Square on 8 July 1776. One block north of Independence Hall is probably Philadelphia's most famous attraction: the Liberty Bell.

Other attractions include the Philadelphia Museum of Art (the 98 steps at the front were made famous in the film *Rocky*). Also worth a visit is the Barnes Foundation which has paintings by Renoir, Cezanne, Matisse, van Gogh, Degas and El Greco.

Just over an hour's drive west of Philadelphia lies the area known as Pennsylvania Dutch Country, home to religious communities such as the Amish, Mennonite and Brethren. The town of Intercourse on Route 340 is a good base for visiting country farms and Amish settlements. The area is also good cycling country.

THE MIDWEST

Chicago and the Great Lakes
'My kinda town', that Toddling Town, the Windy City, the St Valentine's Day Massacre, Al Capone, Upton Sinclair – as much as New York and Los Angeles, Chicago is a leading player in popular American culture. Its huge towering skyscrapers which rear up over Lake Michigan provide the most stunning skylines of any city in the world (including the Sears Tower, at a quarter of a mile high, the tallest building in the world).

Notorious during the Roaring Twenties for the activities of Prohibition racketeers like Capone and Dillinger, Chicago hardly sounds like the sort of place for a jolly family holiday. Don't be misled by *The Untouchables* images generated by Hollywood. Chicago has always been a place of culture (it was, after all, home to architect Frank Lloyd Wright and the place where writer Ernest Hemingway grew up).

There is much for families to do: there is the Chicago Children's Museum on the North Pier, for example, where children can make hand puppets, dress up and take part in a variety of workshops. But nearly all the other museums run special events and programmes for children: from the Art Institute of Chicago (work by Monet and Picasso as well as Grant Woods' famous 'American Gothic' of wife and husband with pitchfork) to the Museum of Science and Industry (which has a full-scale replica of a coal-mine, a Second World War German U-boat and the Apollo 8 spacecraft).

The Great Lakes area with major industrial centres like the motor city of Detroit sounds an unpromising holiday destination. In fact the northern Michigan lakeside area around Traverse City is a major resort area for the Midwest with many elegant resorts and hotels (Harbor Springs, for example, used to be known as the 'Cornbelt Riviera'). For sheer grandeur take a look at the appropriately named Grand Hotel on Mackinac Island. Horton Bay was where Hemingway spent his childhood holidays and which he set his Nick Adams short stories.

Minneapolis/St Paul and Minnesota
Minneapolis and St Paul may be called the Twin Cities but they are certainly not identical twins. St Paul is often called as 'the last

city of the east' because of its grand Victorian buildings and baroque splashes of Art Deco architecture. Minneapolis has a more modern style with modern skyscrapers (fittingly, its most famous son is rock superstar Prince).

Main attractions in Minneapolis include the Minneapolis Institute of Arts, the Walker Art Center, Minnehaha Park (with the Minnehaha Falls featured in Longfellow's poem *Song of Hiawatha*), the extraordinary seven-acre outdoor Sculpture Garden and Minnesota Zoo which offers a koala lodge, camel rides and a beaver exhibit. Shoppers will be keen to visit the Nicollet Mall in Minneapolis which is a mile long.

In St Paul visitors can see the Art Deco City Hall, the Minnesota Museum of Art, the Science Museum of Minnesota and St Paul Cathedral (styled after St Peter's in Rome) with remarkable stained-glass windows. The plush five-mile long Summit Avenue is America's longest expanse of intact residential Victorian architecture: writer F Scott Fitzgerald lived at number 599 where he wrote *This Side of Paradise*.

The state of Minnesota, which has 15,000 lakes and vast areas of unspoilt forest, is perfect country for anyone keen on an active outdoor holiday.

Mount Rushmore and the Great Plains

Places like Dodge City and Deadwood (where Wild Bill Hickok was shot in the back) were the Wild West in the days before people had ventured much beyond the Rocky mountains. Today the stomping grounds of cowboys and indians are in what should be called the Wild Midwest.

The huge Crazy Horse Monument in South Dakota, built as a memorial to the great hero of the American Indian people who defeated General Custer at the Battle of Little Big Horn, was begun by Korczak Ziolkowski in 1948 and even though he died in 1982 his family have continued. When it is finished it will be 563 feet high and 641 feet long.

South Dakota's most famous monument is the Mount Rushmore National Memorial which has the faces of Washington, Roosevelt, Jefferson and Lincoln carved into granite cliffs and surrounded by the pine-covered mountains of the Black Hills. The monument, begun in 1927 and completed 14 years later, was dynamited rather than chiselled out of the rock. Each head stands about 60 feet high.

In Custer State Park, a short drive away, there is an abundance of wildlife including coyotes, antelope, eagles and around 1,500 buffalo (the country's largest publicly-owned herd). It has been estimated that at one time the Great Plains were home to 60 million buffalo – now in America there are just 55,000.

Anyone who has seen *Jurassic Park* or *Dances with Wolves* will be keen to visit the strange landscape of the Badlands which has proved to be a rich source of dinosaur skeletons. Thousands of years of erosion has transformed the treeless landscape into all sorts of bizarre shapes. The Cedar Pass Visitor Center at the entrance to the Badlands National Park has plenty of useful information about the area, with details of hiking trails.

THE SOUTH

Charleston
With more than 1,500 historic buildings (including 200 churches) in just four square miles, Charleston in South Carolina is one of America's loveliest and best preserved cities. Block after block of old buildings has been handsomely restored to commercial and residential use.

The first place to visit is the Visitor Information Center (which has a place to leave your car) where you can learn about how the city has been restored since the thirties as well as providing information on walking tours.

Houses to visit include the Nathaniel Russell House, headquarters of The Historic Charleston Foundation, which is reckoned to be one of America's finest Adam-style buildings. The first shots of the American Civil War were fired at Fort Sumter near Charleston on 12 April 1861 when confederate forces at Fort Johnson opened fire on the Union troops inside Sumter. Park rangers conduct tours of the restored fort.

The sea islands south of Savannah have become major holiday destinations. Kiawah Island, for example, was the location for the 1991 Ryder Cup golf match. Beaufort island, further south, is one of the more unspoilt islands.

Charlottesville and the Shenandoah Valley
America is the land of the automobile where even the hard work gets taken out of sightseeing thanks to the Parkway, a simple two-laned road closed to lorries and farm vehicles with a speed limit of 35mph. Just sit in your car, drive and the view unfolds through the windscreen like a movie (at weekends with the heavy traffic, the movie unfolds a little more slowly!).

The 105-mile Skyline Drive which starts in Front Royal and the Blue Ridge Parkway which runs from Afton for 470 miles down into North Carolina and Tennessee are the perfect way of discovering the Shenandoah Valley. In the woodlands of Shenandoah National Park, the George Washington National Forest and Jefferson National Forest wildcats and black bears can be seen.

Charlottesville, 70 miles west of Richmond, Virginia, is a fine old town with a number of outstanding examples of early American architecture. Three miles south of Charlottesville is Monticello the home of third US President Thomas Jefferson, who wrote the Declaration of Independence. Guided tours take visitors around the house and grounds.

Florida

There is far more to the State of Florida than Disney World and the other attractions of Orlando (see chapter 8). It is indeed a perfect place for a sunshine holiday with a good year round climate. (But watch out for hurricanes in late summer and autumn – and don't be surprised to experience night frosts in late December and January – and most Americans think it's too hot and humid for comfort in high summer...)

Outside the well-known tourist attractions there is another Florida of wildlife reserves, coral reefs and unspoilt islands (and all, if you wish, within a short drive of Miami airport).

Because of the spate of attacks on recently-arrived tourists at the airport – and vivid memories of the TV series *Miami Vice* – Miami has earned a reputation as a dangerous place. There are certainly many places where it is not wise to venture after dark but those who stick to the main tourist areas like Miami Beach, for example, are unlikely to face problems.

One of the best (and safest) parts of Miami is the attractively-restored Art Deco district of South Miami Beach roughly located between fifth and twentieth streets. More than 800 buildings in this small area – less than a square mile – are listed in the National Register of Historic Places. Coconut Grove is said to be the Greenwich Village of South Florida, it was particularly popular with hippies in the sixties. Take a look at the Farmers' Market in Coconut Grove which takes place every Saturday where you can buy home-grown tropical fruits and vegetables, handicrafts, plants and jewellery. Older and posher is Coral Gables which has the distinction of being the first planned community in the United States (take a look at the astonishing Biltmore Hotel). The areas of Little Haiti and Little Havana have a frenetic Caribbean energy about them but in the present climate of anti-tourist aggression are probably best avoided.

South of Miami, the strings of islands known as the Keys are a major holiday destination. The best known and most popular of the islands is Key West, which began to attract celebrity and popularity when writers like Ernest Hemingway and Tennessee Williams settled here. While Key West is now a full-blown holiday resort it has still retained its louche style. The main tourist attraction here (apart from Hemingway's house – now a museum) is to watch the sun go down from Mallory Square.

The Atlantic coast of Florida has the rather brash resort of Fort Lauderdale. Further north is the millionaires' favourite hang-out, Palm Beach. For families however, the principal attraction is the Kennedy Space Center, the headquarters of NASA (National Aeronautics and Space Administration). Get to Spaceport USA early in order to avoid the crowds and enjoy a fascinating tour of the site and its launch pads: a visit to remember.

For beach holidays, without a doubt the Gulf Coast of Florida is the place to head for. For a quiet, almost Caribbean-like holiday, the twin islands of Sanibel and Captiva – reached via Fort Myers – have much to recommend them. Sanibel has an excellent wildlife refuge complete with alligators and eagles. The best beach resorts on the West Coast are Clearwater, St Petersburg and Sarasota (particularly Longboat Key). It is on this stretch of coast that the self-catering brochures feature most of the best houses. A week in Orlando and a week on the Gulf Coast provides the basis for the best Florida fortnight holiday.

Most Florida visitors will want to see the Everglades, the huge area of swampy grassland. The best way to visit is to take Highway 41 to the Shark Alley Visitor Center.

Swimming with the dolphins and manatees

If you want to swim with the dolphins in Florida, the place to head for is the Dolphin Research Center (0101 305 289 0002), on Grassy Key in the Middle Keys of Florida, which is the former home of Milton Santini, creator of the original *Flipper* movie.

Getting to swim with the dolphins needs careful planning since you have to book well in advance (booking opens on the first day of the month before you visit – if you wish to do the swim on 18 March, for example, you will need to make a booking on 1 February). Swimming with the dolphins costs $80 per person, the swim itself lasts 15-20 minutes but the whole 'program' lasts two and a half hours.

If you are keen to swim with loveable sea creatures, your best bet are the manatees. Crystal River, two hours drive north of Tampa, has become the centre of manatee tourism and it guards its manatees jealously. Around 300 manatees – about a quarter of the entire manatee population – are attracted here by the Bay's natural warm springs.

Having been almost wholly indifferent to the fate of these curious creatures for hundreds of years, Florida has suddenly taken a second fancy to them. This fond interest has certainly not been inspired by the manatee's stunning good looks nor its sparkling personality: in appearance it has the face of a particularly stupid labrador dog and the bulging shapeless body mass of a giant slug. You might have thought that it was an unappealing relative of the walrus or a dull second cousin to the seal – but you would be wrong. The manatee is the evolutionary result of some four-footed creature – actually a relative of the elephant – which some 60 million years ago decided that it had had enough of trying to eke out a life on the land and plodded back to the sea.

The manatee is not unique to Florida: there are manatees in West Africa and in the Amazon: it is also closely related to the Australian dugong. But it is in Florida that the manatee has sprung to prominence.

Manatees look ungainly – over 13 feet long and weighing up to more than one and a half tons – but they can move surprisingly quickly when they wish. Unfortunately they do not move as fast as the speedboats with which they regularly collide in the shallow coastal waterways of Florida, usually with fatal consequences for the manatee.

The Lowry Park Zoo in Tampa has one of Florida's four Manatee Hospitals where the sick and injured animals are treated. Recuperated manatees earn their keep by being put on display in a 'Manatee Village' at the zoo. You can watch their underwater existence through large windows while a taped commentary provides information and background.

About half a dozen companies at Crystal River run Swim with the Manatees trips which operate during the winter months from November to March. It is still a relatively low key business, attracting around 15,000 visitors a year. The Crystal River Chamber of Commerce (28 NW Highway 19, Crystal River, Fl 32629, Tel: 904 795 3149) is keen to see the numbers grow. In an effort to promote the manatee connection, the Chamber of Commerce holds a Manatee Festival in Crystal River every February when, for a weekend, the place goes manatee mad.

Further information: Baypoint Diver Center, 300 Highway 19, Crystal River, Fl 34428 (904 563 1040) runs Swim with the Manatee trips for £20 including the use of a wetsuit, flippers, snorkel and mask. Other places to see manatees include Lowry Park Zoo, Tampa (813 935 8552); Homosassa Springs State Wildlife Park (904 628 2311); Sea World of Florida, Orlando (407 363 2355); Miami Seaquarium (305 361 5705).

Great Smoky Mountains National Park
Visitors to this park, lying across the border between Tennessee and North Carolina, receive stern warnings about black bears (they may look tame, but do not be deceived particularly if they have cubs).

The thriving bear community provides evidence of how care-fully this 520,000-acre park is managed. Sixty miles long and twenty miles wide there are reckoned to be more than 200 species of birds living in the park at one time; there are 130 native species of trees (there are 180,000 acres of virgin forest); there are deer, wild turkeys, quail, ruffled grouse, and – of course – the bears.

There are a total of 16 peaks in the park that rise to a height of over 6,000 feet. The mountains get their name from the bluish haze which hangs over them; the reason for the haze is the moisture and hydrocarbons emitted by the plants and trees in the park.

Visitors should start at the Sugarlands Visitor Center at the park entrance (where you can also find the Smoky Mountains National Park headquarters) two miles south of Gatlinburg, Tennessee. If you like walking, consider tackling the Appalachian trail which runs through the park (if you fancy walking the whole trail set aside about seven or eight days).

The major family attraction near the park is Dollywood, located at Pigeon Forge in Tennessee, the theme park owned by country singer Dolly Parton.

The pleasures of a family drive through America
Following the Mississippi from St Louis to New Orleans in the footsteps of Bob Dylan, Paul Simon, Elvis Presley and a juke-box worth of hits...

> *Oh God said to Abraham, 'Kill me*
> *a son.'*
> *Abe says, 'Man, you must be*
> *puttin' me on.'*
> *God say, 'No.' Abe say, 'What?'*
> *God say, 'You can do what you*
> *want Abe, but*
> *The next time you see me comin'*
> *you better run.'*
> *Well Abe says, 'Where do you want*
> *this killin' done?'*
> *'Why, out on Highway 61.'*

Highway 61 Revisited
Bob Dylan

Put away your Rand McNally road atlas of the United States – you could practically drive around America with the lyric sheets of the greatest hits of the fifties and sixties. Like the Aboriginal songlines of the Australian outback, just by reading the American road signs you could sing your way from city to city. Start in St

Louis, for example: head west and you're on the way to Kansas City ('*Well, I'm going to Kansas City, Kansas City here I come*' – Little Richard); south-west lies Route 66 (*it winds through St Louis, Joplin, Missouri...*').

The road south to New Orleans has enough musical themes for a full rock symphony. Paul Simon has passed this way: '*The Mississippi Delta was shining, Like a National Guitar, I am following the river, Down the highway, Through the cradle of the civil war.*' Simon was headed for the Elvis Presley mansion Graceland in Memphis ('*where we have reason to believe we will be received in Graceland, Graceland ...*').

And, of course, there is Highway 61, the road that follows the Mississippi from St Louis to Memphis and down to New Orleans. The road, which actually starts in Bob Dylan's home town of Duluth, Minnesota, must have been a potent symbol for the young and ambitious Robert Zimmerman. Like Jude in Thomas Hardy's *Jude the Obscure* who, as a child, looked longingly towards the cultural lights of Christminster, Dylan must have seen Highway 61 – the road to the music cities of Memphis and New Orleans – as the promise of an imaginatively richer life in the future.

Dylan, lost and alienated in the frigid wastes of Minnesota ('*how does it feel to be on your own, with no direction home?*') could look down this slender highway which stretches north to south across the whole country, towards the southern blacks – the most alienated group of people in America. '*Sam said tell me quick man I got to run, Ol' Howard just pointed with his gun, And said that way down on Highway 61.*

St Louis (it's pronounced Lewis, forget the Judy Garland film) was once a place of promise for the pioneering families who gathered here in the last century to join the wagon trains heading west. A 600 foot high stainless steel arch symbolises this endeavour.

There is little promise offered by the Holiday Inn Riverfront at St Louis: our room on the 24th floor looked as if the last occupants had attacked the nylon carpet with a flame thrower, while the bathroom felt as if someone had recently squeezed an enormous blackhead in it. From our window you could see the large expanse of the Mississippi as it darkly eased its way south ('*Ole Man River, he just keep rollin' along*').

As I checked out of the Holiday Inn, I queried the extra on the bill marked 'Occ Tax'. 'That's an occupancy tax levied by the city,' said the receptionist.

'That's iniquitous,' I remarked.

'Excuse me, sir,' said the receptionist, 'what was that word you just said?'

'Iniquitous?'

'What does that word mean, sir?'

'Evil, I suppose. You know, very bad.'

'Iniquitous: that's a fine word.' She turned to her colleague. 'You know what, Melody: you're iniquitous. You hear that, girl?' The thick dark-framed glasses shook on her nose as she laughed.

Driving in America is a breeze. You go in straight lines (there are no roundabouts), and outside the cities there is little traffic. Being careful to observe the speed limit, give or take 10mph, you switch the radio on, make yourself comfortable, get your motor running and head out on the highway: this is your own personal road movie.

South of St Louis, the countryside repeats itself with an increasing familiarity. Little life seems to exist beyond the main road: development sprawls along either side of the highway with no obvious planning. The big towns have a McDonald's or a Burger King, the smaller ones have a dangerous looking bar and an agricultural machinery dealership. The fields and trees look grey and lifeless. For those who think of America as a wealthy country, the poverty is staggering. An enormous number of people – white and black – seem to live in rickety mobile homes, often gathered together in dilapidated trailer parks.

The only affluent-looking buildings are the churches. Everywhere there are churches with dinky spires and gleaming white picket fences: this is the Bible Belt. When you set the car radio to search for a new station, at least one will be hot gospelling: 'Are you looking for wheels for your emotional luggage? Are you ready to lift the name of the Lord in praise?' Happily there are more rock'n'roll stations, most of them 'bringing you the best of the hits of the sixties and seventies': the Beatles, the Rolling Stones and Bob Dylan are played again and again.

Another surprising thing is the number of dead animals on the side of the road. In Britain you occasionally see the odd squashed hedgehog, and, less frequently, deceased cats: the gutters of Highway 61 teem with all manner of former wildlife. Small dogs, large dogs, things that look like raccoons, huge furry piles that look like small bears, coypu, beaver, skunks (which stink the car out as you pass by).

Highway 61 may follow the Mississippi but the river rarely comes into view. Intrigued by the town of Cairo (pronounced Cay-row), situated in Illinois at the confluence of the Mississippi and Ohio rivers (south of Thebes and north of Memphis) – we took a detour across the river for a brief sweep through Illinois and Kentucky. In Mark Twain's *The Adventures of Huckleberry Finn*, Huck and runaway slave Jim vainly searched for Cairo to seek

Jim's freedom – for, unlike Missouri, slavery had been abolished in Illinois.

The Mississippi was seen as the modern Nile: one supposes that the Egyptian placenames were bestowed as a nod towards the past and an investment of hope in the future. The hope was misplaced; there are no pyramids and no Pharaonic treasures in Cairo; just more sad houses, tired-looking people walking under-nourished dogs, seedy boarding houses and some burnt out shops. Below Cairo we crossed back over the river. Here the Mississippi was a dark, impatient expanse of wild, swirling water that had burst its banks. As far as you could see, forests of anaemic trees stood submerged up to their waists in the muddy water.

Memphis ('*Long distance in formation give me Memphis, Tennessee*' Chuck Berry) promised better things. The Peabody Hotel is an oasis of luxury in the grey poverty of down town Memphis: its fame rests on a party of ducks that by day live in a fountain in the hotel's lobby, and by night reside on the roof. Twice a day, to musical accompaniment, there is a musical parade as the ducks march to and from the elevator. No one says whether the ducks ever waddle their way to the kitchens but, in an appalling gesture of bad taste, duck is a prominent dish on the restaurant menu.

The Peabody is on Union Avenue, a few blocks up from Sun Studios. It was to Sun Studios that a young truck driver called Elvis Presley went to make a recording as a belated Mother's Day present. It was here that the rock'n'roll era is reckoned to have begun, shortly afterwards, when Elvis recorded *That's all right Mama*.

You can have a guided tour of Sun Studios (not much of a tour – it is just one room); the real Presley memorial in Memphis is Graceland. The house has all the style and elegance of an Argos catalogue. Judging by the various additions and 'improvements' made to the house by Presley during his 20-year tenure, it is clear that Elvis was a few tracks short of an LP long before he checked into that Heartbreak Hotel from which no pop singer ever returns.

The guides installed in the various parts of Graceland to point out his bizarre furniture and grotesque light fittings talk in the sort of hushed tones adopted by people ushering pilgrims around the Chapel of the Nativity in Bethlehem. When you are shown Elvis's grave in 'Meditation Garden', you half expect to be told that 'on the third day he rose again'. But then, some say, that is exactly what he did do.

A much more affecting sight in Memphis, just 100 yards from Highway 61, is the Lorraine Motel on Mulberry Street where Martin Luther King was shot dead in 1968. The motel was bought by a local group and turned into a civil rights museum.

Driving south from Memphis, the poverty becomes more and more pronounced. The state of Mississippi is the poorest in America: more shabby trailer parks and flimsy shot-gun shacks. Whites and blacks alike eke out a meagre existence and, with unemployment rising, things are getting worse. But in the South, it seems that the living has never been easy – for the poor, at least. For the rich, life was rather agreeable (as long as you managed to avoid the Mississippi mosquitoes: rich or poor, people here didn't live much beyond the age of 40).

Vicksburg, a few hours' drive south of Memphis, is a Mississippi river town that saw some of the worst fighting of the Civil War. It's the sort of place where you would expect to see people dancing up and down by the river singing 'Showboat coming!' Many of the old *Gone with the Wind* style *antebellum* mansions in the South now earn their living as up-market bed and breakfast guest houses. We stayed at Anchuca, which is not quite Tara but impressive none the less: we had a large room in the slave quarters. 'Ah hope y'all will be real comfortable there,' said our hostess.

We took lunch at a ritzy cafe overlooking the swollen waters of the river. Our waitress clearly thought we were about the oddest people she had ever encountered; we had to repeat everything at least three times before she got the hang of it. By way of conversation I commented on the over-ample state of the river. 'Is it flooding?' I asked. The black waitress looked at me, looked at the surrounding countryside which was 85 per cent under water, and then looked at me again. 'Yeah,' she said with a cackle. 'It done flood.'

The room rate at Anchuca includes breakfast in the formal dining room (grits, of course) and a tour of the house. The Southern accent, as portrayed by Hollywood, sounds as nice as a guinea-pig sharpening its claws on polystyrene. The real thing is delightfully mesmeric. Listening to our hostess as she guided us around the rooms of the mansion, to hear the swooping tone of her voice as vowel sounds were turned around through 180 degrees, was like dozing to a Mozart aria. 'Ah hope y'all come back real soon now,' she said as we left. Out in the garden my wife said she felt like falling to her knees to scrabble in the dirt for some rotten turnips: 'As God is my witness, I'm never going to be hungry again,' she exclaimed. 'Frankly, my dear,' I said, noticing for the first time how much I looked like Clark Gable, 'I don't give a damn.'

The last lap of Highway 61 took us to Baton Rouge and New Orleans. As we left Baton Rouge the radio issued regular 'flash flood advisories'; '100 per cent chance of rain' said the Weather Watch. Indeed the heavens opened and there was 100 per cent rain: as we crossed the causeway to New Orleans on the edge of Lake Pont chartrain, large waves threatened to engulf the road.

New Orleans (pronounced N'Awlins) was dressing itself up in bunting. 'Y'all staying for Mardi Gras?' asked the receptionist at the Marriott. I admitted that I was not. 'Is it fun?' I asked.

'Fun?' she cried: 'It's party time. You like to party?' I admitted that I did not. She clearly found it difficult to handle the concept of people who did not like to party, she probably toyed with the idea of alerting a security guard.

The French Quarter of N'Awlins is like a French or Spanish Mediterranean town transplanted to America. It is the best of taste, it is the worst of taste: it is delightful. I had my picture taken in front of a streetcar named Desire. I had my picture taken in front of a hot dog stand in the shape of a large hot dog (made famous in the John Kennedy Toole book about New Orleans, *A Confederacy of Dunces*). I had a mint julep at Pat O'Brien's bar (a ferocious mixture of bourbon and sugar water). I did not party.

We flew back to London following the line of the Mississippi and Highway 61, stopping at Minneapolis St Paul. A woman who boarded the plane and sat next to me said she was from a small town near Duluth. 'Bob Dylan's birthplace.' I said.

'The pop singer? I didn't know that,' she replied: 'My kids preferred the Beatles.'

Memphis and the Mississippi

Most British tourists who visit Memphis go for one reason: to see Graceland the home and burial place of Elvis Presley. Even for those who aren't the least bit interested in Elvis, Graceland is good kitsch fun and well worth a look if you happen to be passing. Sun Studios, where Elvis recorded his first record as a present for his mother, still operates as a working recording studios but is also open to the public.

Civil rights campaigner Dr Martin Luther King was shot dead at the Lorraine Motel on Mulberry Street on 4 April 1968. The motel has now been converted to a National Civil Rights Museum which tells the story of the black struggle in America.

Music lovers will wish to visit Beale Street reckoned to be the birthplace of the blues. The street was home to W C Handy who published the first blues tunes and played the blues in PeeWee's Saloon.

It has to be said, however, that downtown Memphis is not somewhere to linger for long. By driving south following the mighty Mississippi, you will come to handsome southern towns like Vicksburg and Natchez. Both towns have plenty of Gone with the Wind-style *antebellum* mansions, a number of which offer bed and breakfast accommodation where you can live out your fantasies of being Clark Gable or Vivien Leigh. Vicksburg played a prominent part in the fighting of the American Civil War: in the Vicksburg National Military Park you can see the main battlefield preserved, complete with trenches.

Nashville

A passing interest in country music would help your enjoyment of the city which calls itself the world's Country Music Capital. There is much for the country music fan to enjoy: the Country Music Hall of Fame, the Hank Williams Jr. Museum, Car Collectors Hall of Fame (with one of Elvis's Cadillacs), the Country Music Wax Museum and Mall, the Grand Ole Opry and even Opry Land (not much to do with country music really but a theme park with 21 rides including a terrifying roller-coaster).

Despite the glitz and the tack, Nashville likes to play up its serious side. It also calls itself the Athens of the South, and to support this claim it has built a replica of the Athens Parthenon (right down to the Elgin Marbles).

New Orleans

The Big Easy, as this Louisiana city is called, has an atmosphere and style unique in America. It is a place that looks and feels more like somewhere you would find on the Mediterranean than on the Gulf of Mexico. The residents of New Orleans are unashamedly devoted to the concept of enjoying themselves (their motto is *laissez les bon temps rouler*: let the good times roll). The New Orleans good times roll fastest every year during its Mardi Gras festival when six million visitors come to watch the weird and wonderful carnival floats and drink too many mint juleps.

The tourist centre of the city is the French Quarter with its blocks of houses with overhanging ironwork balconies. The main thoroughfare is the intriguingly tacky Bourbon Street full of bars and music clubs. The centre of the Quarter is Jackson Square, once the place where public executions were held, now a place for New Orleans en fete.

New Orleans is the city where jazz was born, with the music performed by legendary artists like Louis Armstrong and Joe 'King' Oliver. There are many jazz clubs in the city but the most famous place to see traditional jazz played is the Preservation Hall on St Peter Street.

Within driving distance of New Orleans in southern Louisiana is Cajun Country, a land of swamps and bayous and home to the Acadians who were expelled by the British from Canada in 1755. The best place to see Cajun music played is in and around Lafayette.

Washington DC

As the capital of the United States and the seat of government, you would be forgiven for thinking that Washington was rather a dull place that can be dropped from your itinerary. In fact Washington is one of the best family holiday places in America. Everybody will enjoy looking at the White House (get there before 8am to join the queue for a free of charge tour ticket: tours operate Tuesday to Saturday).

Get a ticket for the Tourmobile bus which will take you around the main sights (the ticket is valid all day and you can get on and off as much as you wish). The Tourmobile circuit includes the Capitol, the Washington Monument, the Jefferson Memorial, the Lincoln Memorial, the Vietnam Veterans' Memorial and Arlington National Cemetery where assassinated president John F Kennedy is buried. Arrange your journey so that you can stop at the magnificently restored Union Station for lunch (in the basement there is a superb array of eateries).

It is the museums which most families will enjoy most. The National Air and Space Museum is stunning: with the Wright Brothers' plane that made the first powered flight, the Spirit of St Louis in which Charles Lindbergh made the first transatlantic solo flight and a piece of real moon rock that you can touch. In the National Museum of American History you can see an extraordinary collection of artefacts: the ruby slippers worn by Judy Garland in the film version of *The Wizard of Oz*, the leather jacket worn by the Fonz in the TV sitcom *Happy Days*, Muhammad Ali's boxing gloves and the original Star Spangled Banner which inspired America's national anthem.

Also good fun is a tour of the FBI (Federal Bureau of Investigation) where groups can study the list of the 10 most wanted criminals, look at forensic and bullet-testing laboratories followed by a live-firing display (not for the nervous!).

Ford's Theatre, where President Lincoln was shot, has been restored to the way it looked on 14 April 1865 on the night of the assassination. The gun and fatal bullet can be seen in the theatre's basement.

About two hours' drive south of Washington is Colonial Williamsburg, a handsomely restored and cleverly reconstructed living museum, presenting a vivid representation of how the Virginian capital would have looked at the time immediately before the American Revolution in the 1770s.

THE WEST

California

In many ways California is the perfect family holiday destination. Florida has the fun parks but beyond Miami lacks little in the way of real life. California, however, has it all: in fact following the 1992 Rodney King riots it could be said that there is too much real life.

For many people the state of California sums up the glamorous allure of America. Los Angeles, with the Hollywood studios and theme parks like Disneyland; the stunning good looks of San Francisco; the wine country of Napa and Sonoma Valleys; Death Valley; Yosemite Valley; San Diego (and the frontier with Mexico); and all played to a sound-track of Beach Boy music promising an endless summer of sun, fun and surf.

Los Angeles is not really a single place, more a huge collection of towns (it's described as 'nineteen suburbs in search of a city'). You have to drive from end to end (a distance of some 50 miles) to realise just how much it sprawls. It is a place built for the motor car (seen from the air the highways and freeways criss-cross and interweave like a giant jumble of spaghetti).

It is undoubtedly an exciting place. There is a thrill at the first glimpse of the Hollywood sign, the fun of driving down Sunset Boulevard (look out for the famous Beverly Hills Hotel), seeing the Mann's Chinese Theatre outside which stars' hand and foot prints are immortalised in cement. For a glimpse of Hollywood, Universal Studios runs a tour that supposedly offers some back-stage glimpses but which is really more of a theme park experience – serious cineastes should take the Burbank Studios tour.

Disneyland in Anaheim was the original Disney theme park, and many would argue that it remains the best (it is on a more human scale than the massive Disney World in Florida). There are other theme parks: Knott's Berry Farm in Buena Park; Raging Waters in San Dimas ('44 lush acres and five million gallons of water...'); and Six Flags Magic Mountain which has some of the most terrifying roller-coaster rides in the world.

North of LA, near Santa Monica, is the J Paul Getty Museum, a sort of artistic theme park. In an impressive reproduction Roman villa can be seen an extraordinary array of art treasures. Paintings on view include works by Rubens, Goya, Breughel, Canaletto and Van Gogh's Irises.

Around 130 miles south of LA, San Diego has rapidly become the second biggest city in California but is often overlooked as a holiday destination. It not only has 70 miles of excellent sandy Pacific beaches, with its zoo and Sea World the city has two of the finest family outings in the whole of America. The zoo in Balboa

Park has over 3,000 creatures and a 40-hectare tropical garden. Sea World on Mission Bay has six separate sea animal shows (the most famous performer is Shamu, the killer whale), there is also the world's largest exhibit of penguins. From San Diego it's a brief drive across the border to Tijuana in Mexico (not the greatest shop window for Mexico, it has to be said): check that your car insurance allows you to drive your car over the frontier.

Route One, the Pacific Coast Highway, is the 400-mile road to take from Los Angeles up to San Francisco (it's often a slow, winding road not for people in a hurry: if you want to be quick take the Interstate 101). The Highway takes you through Malibu, Santa Barbara, up Big Sur and the Monterey Peninsula. The coastal views are usually never less than stunning (the 17 Mile Drive on the Monterey Peninsula is particularly magnificent).

The actual driving will take around 10 hours but you could easily spend a few days seeing all the sights en route. You will want to see Hearst Castle, the lavish residence of newspaper magnate William Randolph Hearst, the model for Orson Welles' *Citizen Kane*. You should also linger in Carmel, where Clint Eastwood was once mayor. Cannery Row in Monterey, once a squalid neighbourhood of warehouses and slums, is now a handsome shopping complex.

San Francisco is without doubt America's most romantic city. The sight of the Golden Gate Bridge striding across the bay is one of the greatest views in the world. The city itself, while big (and with plenty of steep hills) is a good place for walkers (whenever you get weary, hop aboard a cable car or take a bus or underground train – San Francisco's public transport system is very impressive). The main sights include Fisherman's Wharf, Golden Gate Park and the boat ride across to Alcatraz Island where you can take a tour of the prison which housed the famous Birdman and the infamous Al Capone.

Whereas it is hard (some would say impossible) to get to the heart of Los Angeles, the centre of San Francisco is a vibrant, energetic place. Check out Chinatown, for example, with its teeming bazaars and restaurants. You will discover how easy it is to leave your heart in San Francisco.

Mountain bike enthusiasts should head north across the Golden Gate Bridge to Marin County where the mountain bike was first developed (not surprisingly perhaps the countryside around here provides ideal mountain biking territory). If you want to see the exact spot where the mountain bike was developed go to the little town of Fairfax, Marin County, California and ride up Mount Tamalpais. The mountain bike did not come about as a result of a major corporation spending millions on developing a new product. This hi-tech machine emerged in the mid-1970s, when a bunch of California hippies souped up old bikes to see who could get down the hill the fastest.

The most famous race came to be known as the Repack, because the grease in the powerful drum brakes on the old Clunker cycles they used would turn to smoke, meaning they would have to be re-packed after each race. The Clunker bikes gradually metamorphosed into the slick mountain bikes we know today. On Mount Tamalpais there is a trail called The Repack Road clearly marked on the maps, but the races no longer take place. Strict speed limits enforced by park rangers restrict the mountain tracks to cyclists who wish to travel at a more leisurely pace.

Other good cycling country well worth exploring is to be found among the vineyards of the Napa Valley and Sonoma.

In inland California lie Redwood National Park famous for its giant trees which reach nearly 350 feet, and Yosemite National Park which has more remarkable flora (including its own impressive sequoia trees including the 2,700 year old Grizzly Giant). There are plenty of hiking and biking trails. Death Valley is worth a trip if only because it is reckoned to be the hottest place on earth, so clearly not the sort of place to be wandered into without a certain degree of preparation.

Grand Canyon
This is one of the Seven Great Natural Wonders of the World. Film and photographs do not prepare you for the sight of this extraordinary geological phenomenon which runs for 227 miles, 17 miles across at its widest point and over a mile deep at its deepest point.

The South Rim, about two hours' drive from Flagstaff, Arizona, is the most visited part of the Canyon receiving 90 per cent of the three million tourists who visit the Grand Canyon every year. The North Rim, about five hours' drive from Flagstaff, is much less developed and worth the extra drive.

The Grand Canyon can be visited in a variety of ways. Take a mule ride down the side of the gorge, descend by helicopter, travel through the rapids on a white-water raft, or you could just see it all by foot.

Las Vegas
America's gambling capital may seem an improbable place for a family holiday, however there is more to the city than one-armed bandits, roulette tables and drive-in wedding ceremonies.

There is plenty of accommodation (the city has nine of the world's ten largest hotels) and much of it at half the price charged in other places (rooms are subsidised by gambling profits). For breakfast you will find all-you-can-eat buffets for as little as £1.50.

On the Strip you will find the famous hotels like The Mirage, Caesars Palace and the Sands. Children will enjoy Circus Circus where trapeze artists are employed to perform over the heads of gamblers! To cool off from the blistering desert heat, Wet'n'Wild is a 26-acre water park full of pools and all sorts of water slides.

New Mexico
Not so long ago New Mexico was a state that travellers raced through en route to somewhere else (the famous Route 66 took people between Chicago and LA). One of the reasons people might not wish to linger was that atomic bombs were tested here.

But in the past five years New Mexico has become synonymous with good style. Santa Fe and its near neighbour Taos, 60 miles to the north, offer an excellent year-round climate and a culture that blends Native American, Spanish and what they call Anglo (a local term describing anybody who is not Native American or Spanish!).

The area has long attracted writers and artists. D H Lawrence lived here (some of his paintings which were banned in London can be seen in the manager's office of La Fonda de Taos Hotel in Taos).

Denver and the Rocky Mountain National Park
Denver's greatest attraction is its proximity to the Rocky Mountains. Known as the Mile High City, it is one mile above sea level, Denver has few major attractions (one of the main sights is the home of the Unsinkable Molly Brown, a survivor of the Titanic (and the subject of a musical film starring Debbie Reynolds).

Boulder, 27 miles north-west of Denver, is probably a better base for exploring the Rockies: there are a number of places here where you can hire mountain bikes. The Rocky Mountains National Park provides the visitor with a magnficent slice of scenery and offers some magnificent walks. Animals in the park include moose, coyote, mountain lions, beavers and brown bears.

In Colorado are the ski resorts most popular with British holiday-makers: places like Breckenridge, Aspen and Vail are smart and efficient, with good snow.

Seattle
This city in the north-west corner of America has been best known as the place where Boeing makes its aircraft. But in the last couple of years, Seattle has been attracting an increasing number of holiday-makers who enjoy its agreeable year-round climate, its attractive parks and easy access to walking trails and cycle paths.

Like many cities on the West Coast it has a large Asian population: particularly Chinese and Filipino, which means there are a good range of Oriental restaurants and shops, and places offering acupuncture and massage.

Main tourist sights include the Museum of Flight, located in the Red Barn, the original Boeing aircraft factory and the tall Space Needle.

Texas

When the TV series *Dallas* was at the height of its popularity several years ago, Texas enjoyed a mini-boom in tourism from Britain. Since the departure of *Dallas*, Texas seems to have dropped off the tourist itinerary. This is a pity because there is much more to Texas than J R Ewing.

It is certainly big: 800 miles from east to west, almost 1,000 miles from top to bottom: room for the whole of France, Belgium, Switzerland and the Netherlands put together. It could easily be a country all on its own: in fact, for nine years from 1836 to 1845 it was.

Dallas will probably be forever associated with the assassination of John F Kennedy who was shot dead in the city on 22 November 1963. The room on the sixth floor of the Texas School Book Depository, from which it is believed the fatal shot was fired, now houses a small museum.

Houston will be forever associated with space flight and moon landings (as in 'Houston – this is Tranquility Base, the Eagle has landed': the first message radioed back from the surface of the moon). The Space Center Houston, 25 miles south-east of the city centre, offers enough amusement and entertainment to keep children occupied for hours.

Texas's main holiday area is on the Gulf Coast which offers almost one thousand miles of shoreline made up of bays, barrier islands and river deltas. The main holiday places include Galveston which has the excellent Texas Seaport Museum and a Railroad Museum.

From Rockport-Fulton you can travel out to view the whooping cranes and the other wildlife in the Arkansas Wildlife Refuge. Corpus Christi is a centre for a watersports.

Yellowstone National Park

This is the one American National Park that most British people have heard of (if only because it provided the model for Jellystone Park in the Yogi Bear cartoon series!). The park is an astonishing place: in its area – about 60 miles by 50 miles – are more than half the geysers in the world. The most famous geyser is Old Faithful which sends out a plume of water roughly every 65-78 minutes.

You will see elk in the park, and also grizzly bears (but probably not Yogi Bear).

Alaska
It has to be said that Alaska is not the first place travellers would consider for a holiday, let alone a family holiday. But for those with a passion for the outdoors and for keen naturalists, the state is a destination worth considering. Bear in mind that Alaska is very big (incredibly, it is twice the size of Texas).

The most popular holiday destination situated north of Anchorage is the Denali National Park, a six million-acre wilderness area in which can be found Mt McKinley, the highest mountain on the North American continent. During the summer a free bus service operates an 80-mile journey through the park allowing visitors to see a wide variety of wildlife including brown bears, caribou and moose. Dog-sled demonstrations are held in the park. The Nenana River in the park offers good whitewater rafting with a number of operators providing trips.

Travellers to the state capital Juneau or to Valdez can take cruises to look at glaciers, and see whales and porpoises.

Hawaii
America's Fiftieth State (something we all know from the *Hawaii Five-O* TV series) is situated over two thousand miles out in the Pacific Ocean from the American mainland. It is every American's idea of the perfect holiday destination: golden palm-fringed beaches, pounding surf, lush vegetation, smart resorts – a tropical world, but an all-American one.

There are 162 Hawaiian islands of which 7 are inhabited. The biggest of the islands, twice the size of all the other islands combined, is Hawaii – known as The Big One.

The principal holiday destination of Hawaii is on the island of Oahu: the city of Honolulu and the resort area of Waikiki beach. The two major tourist attractions are Pearl Harbor, attacked by the Japanese on 7 December 1941 bringing America into the Second World War. Visitors can learn about the events of that fateful day at the *USS Arizona* Memorial. The Monument straddles the hulk of the *USS Arizona* which sank with 1,102 men on board.

You can also walk to the summit of Diamond Head, a dormant volcano. A tunnel takes you through the crater's wall: from here it's a three-quarters of a mile walk to the summit. The views of Waikiki from the summit are sensational.

8

A WEEK IN ORLANDO

The British love Orlando. Not since the sixties when we first discovered Benidorm, Torremolinos and Magaluf, have we encountered a holiday place quite so much to our taste. We love it because in most respects it is almost the complete opposite to Britain. The weather is good, the streets are cleaned, the living is easy and cheap, the citizens are cheerful. It is a slice of wholesome America familiar from James Stewart films.

Orlando is a city wholly dedicated to providing pleasure. It is a place created by tourism. In the time BD (Before Disney) Orlando was a hick town of citrus groves and murky mangrove swamps: the area was known as Mosquito County. And then Walt created Disney World. As early as 1958 Walt Disney had decided to search for a site to build a second, much bigger Disneyland. Disney had confounded his critics with the successful opening of the first Disneyland in Anaheim, California in 1955.

In November 1963 Walt flew to Florida to take an aerial look at potential sites for his second park. After circling above the forests and swamps of Orlando in a light aircraft to check the lie of the land, his party returned to New Orleans airport where they discovered everybody gathered around televisions and radios. President Kennedy had just been shot in Dallas. The Disney party returned to California in gloomy silence, anxious that the project might have been born under a bad sign.

The whole plan did seem ridiculously over-ambitious. Walt ordered a clandestine scheme to acquire 27,000 acres of mostly swamp-land property near Orlando at a price of around $180 per acre. The purchase was carried out through third parties because Disney was convinced that if his name was linked with the deal, property prices would spiral. He was right: when the Disney connection was finally revealed land prices in the area shot up to $1000 an acre. (Nowadays, even during the current recession, purchasers will have to pay $125,000 an acre).

On 1 October 1971, 100,000 visitors were expected for opening day: in fact, only 10,000 turned up and Disney stock immediately slumped on Wall Street. It turned out to be Disney World's worst ever day: daily visitor numbers were never so low again – even during a hurricane, 20,000 visitors still manage to get through the turnstiles of the Magic Kingdom.

In 1982 Disney followed up with the second part of Walt's dream: EPCOT – his Experimental Prototype Community of Tomorrow. He had planned a sort of Dan Dare city of the future – a community under a hermetically sealed glass dome where people could live in harmony with the world. What opened to the public was much less ambitious – more a permanent World's Fair with rides, exhibitions and a 'world showcase'.

The early eighties were a difficult time for Disney: without Walt's leadership the company lost its touch in movie-making and the potential of the theme parks was not realised. Under the new management of Michael Eisner and Frank Wells, who took over in 1984, Disney rediscovered its magic touch. Disney-MGM Studios was the company's third attraction to open in Orlando in 1989 – and the company embarked on an orgy of hotel and property development to capitalize on its extensive land ownership.

Disney's new enthusiasm was largely motivated by the fact that other hotel groups and tourist attractions had cashed in on the foundations it had laid for Orlando's success. Since 1971 the area had seen the setting up of dozens of tourist attractions from Sea World to the Elvis Presley Museum.

Through the last half of the eighties, tourism to Orlando boomed in a spectacular fashion. In 1980 Orlando received 4.6m visitors – by 1984 this total had grown fairly modestly to 5.6m visitors; but over six years later by 1991 the number had increased almost threefold to 13.6m.

In order to keep pace with visitor numbers, over the past decade property developers have been constructing new hotels in Orlando with impressive energy. Since 1986 the number of hotel rooms in the Metro Orlando area has increased by almost 50 per cent from 57,800 to over 77,000. The area of Metro Orlando has the largest concentration of hotel rooms in the United States, more than even New York or Los Angeles.

Five years ago, British visitors were routinely assumed to be Australian or even Canadian. Nowadays in Orlando, the locals have learnt to identify the Brits if not by their accents then at least by the ubiquitous shell suit. Many tourist shops on Highway 192 stock copies of the previous day's *Sun*, *Mirror* and *Mail*. English pubs, complete with wideboy English landlords swathed in gold jewellery, proliferate along Highway 192. And there are takeaway Indian restaurants and several shops where addicts can buy a fix of Jacob's Cream Crackers or a tin of Quality Street.

In a 1989 survey, of the 1.9m overseas visitors to Orlando, the UK was the single biggest market accounting for 38 per cent of the total – the nearest European contender was Germany with

119

seven per cent. At Disney World, British visitors recently overtook Canadians as the leading foreign market. Wherever you go in Disney, from the Pirates of the Caribbean to The Great Movie Ride, English accents are regularly overheard.

Many Brits are buying holiday homes: new substantial three-bedroom houses with heated pools, air-conditioning and integral garages, in locations just five minutes from the entrance to Disney World, can be bought for as little as £60,000. (Real estate agents describe with amazement how Brits arrive at their offices with money stuffed in a suitcase.) Many of these British-owned houses are then re-let to British holidaymakers for as little as £400 per week. (The Americans seem less well disposed to the idea of self-catering on holiday.)

Attacks on British and other foreign tourists in Orlando and Florida has undoubtedly hit bookings over the past 12 months. However it seems certain that demand will recover. The British love affair with Orlando has probably only just begun.

An Orlando strategy

The secret to a successful holiday in Orlando is careful planning. It may sound a bit cool and calculating for something as spontaneous and jolly as a holiday but the more effort you put into organising the trip, the more enjoyment you get out of it. The organization is needed largely because for a truly good time in Orlando you have to beat the crowds. On an August day there are likely to be at least 250,000 other people in Orlando keen to see and do the same things as you (expect to run up against at least 80,000 in the Disney parks). The trick is to outmanoeuvre them.

One of the main weapons in your armoury will be *The Unofficial Guide to Walt Disney World* (TUGTWDW) by Bob Sehlinger (Simon & Schuster, £6.99). He will tell you, for example, that the worst days to go to the Magic Kingdom are Monday, Tuesday and Wednesday (everybody flies into Orlando on a Sunday and goes straight to Space Mountain on Monday morning).

Travellers need to buy TUGTWDW several weeks before they get to Orlando and swot up on its instructions and recommendations. It will tell you which rides are best for which age groups. Which rides have the fastest throughputs and therefore the fastest-moving queues (the Pirates of the Caribbean can handle thousands of people an hour while Dumbo, the Flying Elephant can take only dozens in an hour).

TUGTWDW will sort out the bulk of your Orlando holiday which will inevitably focus on Walt Disney World. Out of an average holiday of seven days, visitors will probably want to allocate four or five days to Disney: one each for the Magic Kingdom, EPCOT, and Disney-MGM, devoting the remaining days to the excellent water parks Typhoon Lagoon and River Country – and to revisiting favourite rides and attractions.

The success of the TUGTWDW depends on rising each day at around 6am and returning home for lunch and an afternoon rest, and returning to the parks for the evening fun: electric parades, fireworks etc which take place until well into the night. It can be a hard, tiring schedule – particularly for young children – which is why you probably do need five days to see it all comfortably.

TUGTWDW also has plenty of good advice on where to stay to get the most out of Disney. On-the-lot hotels are probably worth the extra expense because you don't have to spend a lot of time and trouble travelling backwards and forwards from your hotel to Disney. The last two times we've been to Orlando, we've stayed in self-catering places. The best was a magnificent three-bedroom house with its own pool in splendid isolation about five minutes' drive from the Magic Kingdom car park: it cost £400 for a week (see the self-catering chapter for a listing).

To help your planning these are my recommendations (if you disagree with my opinions, please let me know!):

WALT DISNEY WORLD (407-824 4321)

Nothing irks the Disney organization as much as people who say that something is 'Mickey Mouse' meaning that it's sub-standard or badly organized. Because if Disney prides itself on anything, then it is the quality of its organization. Walt Disney World which straddles 28,000 acres of central Florida is the very model of organization: this is definitely no Mickey Mouse set-up.

If the place gleams with cleanliness and good order, it isn't because Disney visitors are suddenly imbued with Boy Scout neatness. It's because a hefty part of the 32,000 Disney workforce here spend all day sweeping up the Mouseketeer ice-cream wrappers, popcorn boxes and Coke cartons. No employee, not even an executive vice-president, is allowed to walk past a piece of rubbish without putting it into the nearest bin.

At EPCOT there are men dressed in beau geste outfits who seem to spend hour after hour simply circling the lake on their hands and knees with a spray bottle in one hand and a metal chisel in the other, scraping up the jellyfish gobs of chewing gum. Not only scraping up the chewing gum, but doing it with fun and enthusiasm – as if this was the job they had been preparing for all their lives.

These people on their hands and knees in the burning sun aren't just street cleaners – they're in show business. At Disney employees aren't employees, they're 'cast members' – the place where staff are recruited is called 'casting' – and they are instructed to perform: Disney World, they are told, is larger than life. One day you're out there in the gunge prising up the Wrigley's Spearmint, the next they could be hanging a star on your dressing-room door. It's show biz.

It might all be a line from *Mary Poppins*, one of Disney's big successes: *'In every job that must be done, there is an element of fun, you find the fun and – snap! – the job's a game...'*

In the Kingdom of Disney, cleanliness is right up there next to profitability. When visitors are asked what they like best about Disney World – and why they want to come back – the reason that people give most often is that the place is so clean. No rubbish, and by extension no graffiti, no muggings, no rapes: inside the Magic Kingdom, life is the way we would all like it to be, safe and squeaky clean.

(Don't listen to the 'urban myths' which circulate about children being snatched from Disney World by trained gangs of South American kidnappers never to be seen again. These heart-rending tales are silly horror stories with not the slightest element of truth about them.)

Creating the Disney feel-good atmosphere takes a lot of work. New recruits from executive vice-presidents down to toilet attendants sit side by side at the Disney University where they learn the rules of the Disney game. No facial hair for the men, no eyeshadow, dangling earrings or coloured stockings for the women – if you're too overweight or too short you won't be allowed to appear in public but put to work behind the scenes.

'It's a conservative company,' said one 'cast member': 'We're told that before we come.' But if the rules are tough, Disney is reckoned to be a generous – and very fair – employer. Management employees, for example, even the most senior ones, have to put on a 'character costume' and find out for themselves what life is like on the streets of the Magic Kingdom. Dressing up in a claustrophobic Robin Hood costume and having 30 kids charge at you is a sobering reminder of the business that Disney is engaged in.

But from the tram driver who takes you from the car park ('Hi, I'm Bob your driver: I want you folks to remember you're parked in the Goofy section of our parking lot...') right through to the queue supervisors on the Jungle Cruise ride ('You guys from Texas? Anyone from Texas here...? Yo, awright!!!'), the enthusiasm is blistering.

The organization of the queuing has been refined to an art. The lines of people are threaded up, down, back and forward to keep them moving and make the wait look as short as possible – often you reach what you thought was the front of the queue only to discover you are in a 'pre-waiting' or 'pre-entertainment' area. Signs that say 'from this point the waiting time is 60 minutes' are put at places where the waiting time is really 45 minutes – so that when you get to the end of the queue you are delighted that you had to wait *only* 45 minutes instead of an hour.

Disney has been particularly conscious of its lack of appeal to thrill-seeking American post-pubescents who find the Disney style rather too 'Pollyanna' for their New Kids on the Block tastes. To appeal to this age group Disney has opened new rides (the terrifying Splash Mountain) as well as a sophisticated water fun park Typhoon Lagoon – and for night-time fun it has built Pleasure Island, with a choice of discos, night-clubs, a 'Rocker RollerDome' and the Comedy Warehouse.

And new attractions at the theme parks are taking a more adult approach. Even sex rears its ugly head at the new 'Wonders of Life' pavilion at EPCOT which features a film *The Making of Me*: 'The mysterious, wonderful and often funny process of pregnancy and birth...' Don't expect *Deep Throat* – more like Deeply Embarrassing.

The massive programme of investment has produced a crop of extraordinary new hotels on the Disney property. Leading post-modernist California architect Michael Graves has produced a magnificent pair of adjacent hotels, the 758-room Swan and the 1509-room Dolphin, at a combined cost of £250 million. The witty, confident design of the hotels is visible evidence of the new confidence and energy of the Disney corporation.

There are plans for continuing expansion. There is talk of a fourth theme park at Orlando – and more attractions for the existing parks. The Disney plan is to create something that positively overwhelms the visitor, so that he ends up feeling that no matter how hard he tries he will never see it all. No matter how big your expectations are, they will always be exceeded.

What to expect

People who have never been to Disney World probably imagine it as some sort of hi-tech fairground park with roller-coasters, water-splashes and haunted houses – but all done with that smart, sophisticated Disney twist. The heart of the Disney World concept, the Magic Kingdom – largely a replica of the original Disneyland in Anaheim near Los Angeles – offers a variety of what are indeed essentially fairground thrills.

But to call 'The Pirates of the Caribbean' a water-splash – or to say that 'Space Mountain' is simply a roller-coaster is rather like saying that Van Gogh was a dab hand at painting sunflowers. But the best of the Magic Kingdom rides are practically works of art. The vivid night sky that broods over the sea battle in 'The Pirates of the Caribbean', for example, is in its way, as breath-taking as a Michelangelo ceiling in the scale of its execution.

But there is more, much more to Disney World than the Magic Kingdom. There is also EPCOT (Experimental Prototype Community of Tomorrow) and the newest addition, Disney-MGM Studios. Each of these on their own is a considerable attraction in its own right – to see everything in all three would take even the most enthusiastic visitor at least a week.

Good for children?

You see a lot of small children at Disney World, for whom the experience, far from being a delight, turns out to be a terrible ordeal. Children need to be at least seven years old to get the maximum enjoyment. The crowds, the heat, and the sometimes alarming nature of the special effects – even on the 'mellow' rides – can be overwhelming for much older kids.

It's interesting to note that while most people claim that they go to Disney World 'for the kids', adults outnumber children by four to one. It may be hard to believe, yet Disney World has now displaced Niagara as America's leading honeymoon destination.

Planning your visit

Organizing a successful trip to Disney World calls for precision planning. The time of year you visit will be probably fixed by other factors (your children's school holidays, for example), but if you have a choice, the times to avoid Disney World are Christmas and New Year, the second and third weeks of April, and from the second week of June to the third week of August. The quietest time is from September to Christmas, with the exception of the Thanksgiving holiday period at the end of November.

The days of the week you choose to visit Disney World are important. The busiest days (up to 150,000 visitors) are Monday and Tuesday, (most visitors arrive in Orlando on a Sunday and start their visit on a Monday). The quietest days (25,000) are Friday, Saturday and Sunday (with the exception of public holiday weekends). On a 'quiet' day, there will be 25,000 visitors: on a busy day, up to 150,000. Since most of the Disney attractions are 'rides', queuing is usually inevitable particularly for the most popular rides. On busy days the queues can stretch for an hour or more – on quiet days, or at quiet times of days, queues can be non-existent.

A plan of attack

You are not going to be able to see everything in the three parks in four days, so you need to decide in advance what you want to do. For each of the three parks, Disney produces excellent free guides with good maps that show where all the attractions are and also mark the eating places and toilets.

For each of the parks decide in advance which rides you want to do first (see below for my recommendations) and enjoy these as quickly as possible. Then explore the rest of the park, trying as many rides as you can comfortably manage. Remember that all the rides and nearly all of the other attractions are included in the price of admission. You can travel on them again and again as often as you wish – for as long as you have the stamina. Disney World is hot year-round, but in summer from May to October the strong sun and high humidity can make the going difficult, particularly for children. It is worth going early simply to beat the worst of the heat.

By arriving at the parks early – aim on parking your car at least 45 minutes before the scheduled opening time – you can avoid the worst of the heat and also miss the crowds, even on the busiest days. Finish by around mid-day, get your hand stamped for re-entry and return to your hotel for lunch, a swim and a short nap. Go back to the park for the late afternoon and stay for as long as you can manage: it's worth staying for any evening entertainment such as fireworks or the marvellous Electric Parade in the Magic Kingdom.

There are lots of restaurants and fast-food places in Disney World, but apart from the occasional snack or ice-cream, you would be better advised to eat elsewhere. In all the parks there are lots of chilled water fountains – drink as often as possible.

Magic Kingdom
This the park that most people associate with Disney World. Here you will find the well-known landmark of Cinderella Castle standing at the end of Main Street with its old-fashioned buses and horse-drawn trolleys.

Main Street, with its shops and eating places, is open up to an hour before the official opening time of the park. If the official opening time is 9am, try to get to Main Street by around 8.30am about half an hour before and be ready to head for the rides as soon as the rope is dropped at the end of Main Street.

The Magic Kingdom is the most exhausting of the Disney parks. Just reaching the main entrance is a marathon. You park your car, are taken by what they call a tram to the ticket area, from where you then travel on to the park itself by either ferry boat or monorail (for speed choose the monorail).

The park is divided into four main 'lands': Adventureland, Frontierland and Liberty Square, Fantasyland and Tomorrowland, all of which lead off the Central Plaza in front of Cinderella Castle.

These are the main rides which you should try first:

The Pirates of the Caribbean (Adventureland): This will offer a marvellous introduction to the wonders of Disney World – a night-time boat ride through a pirate attack on a Caribbean sea port.

Big Thunder Mountain Railroad(Frontierland): A roller-coaster ride on a runaway train through an old gold-rush mining town. (Children below a minimum height not admitted.)

Splash Mountain (Adventureland): State-of-the-art flume ride with a terrifying vertical drop.

Haunted Mansion (Liberty Square): Outstanding ghostly special effects (even a ghost hitch-hiking a ride in your car), but amusing rather than terrifying.

Space Mountain (Tomorrowland): The biggest and the best of the roller-coaster rides – and all mostly in the dark. When they say this ride isn't suitable for people with weak hearts, you had better believe them. (Children below a minimum height not admitted.)

With the exceptions of 'Space Mountain' and 'Splash Mountain', (younger people of a nervous disposition will find them too alarming), most children can enjoy all of the above. Younger children will enjoy most of the rides in Fantasyland: 'Mad Tea Party' (travel in giant teacups), 'Mr Toad's Wild Ride', 'Dumbo', 'It's a Small World' and 'Peter Pan's Flight'. Adjacent to Fantasyland is Mickey's Birthdayland where children can join in a 'surprise' birthday party and afterwards meet Mickey 'backstage' in his dressing room. Older children will enjoy driving a racing car – albeit at a maximum 5mph – on the Grand Prix Raceway. For adults, another ride to try if you have the time and if the queue is reasonable, is 'The Jungle Cruise' (Adventureland).

Disney-MGM Studios

This is the newest of the Disney World theme parks and, in many ways, the best. It is certainly the most compact: there is less walking to be done than in the others. Another big major advantage is that if you get here early enough, you can walk to the entrance from the car park without having to go by tram.

The Great Movie Ride: Arrive early and start at the replica of the famous Hollywood Chinese Theatre at the end of 'Hollywood Boulevard', where you will begin your journey on 'The Great Movie Ride'. This is a ride through several 'AudioAnimatronic' robot set-pieces of great Hollywood moments – John Wayne, Tarzan, *Aliens, The Wizard of Oz*, Humphrey Bogart and Ingrid Bergman from *Casablanca* – but be prepared for surprising live action as well. I challenge you to watch the final montage of classic Hollywood film-clips and not shed a tear or two.

Star Tours: One of the latest Disney attractions, this is a simulated spaceship ride, Star Wars-style, with a probationer pilot at the controls. The effects are astonishingly realistic, and also very funny – but it is definitely not for the faint-hearted.

Indiana Jones Epic Stunt Spectacular: Impressively slick recreation of Indiana Jones film stunts, climaxing with the famous fight on the moving aircraft with accompanying explosions and fire so big and hot it practically burns your cheeks. People are chosen from the audience to participate in the action: hide under your seat if you look like being picked out. (This is the show that the Princess of Wales, William and Harry enjoyed so much on their Disney trip in Summer 1993.)

SuperStar Television: Without doubt the funniest attraction in Disney World: through the wonders of modern technology members of the audience are able to star in *The Lucy Show, Cheers, General Hospital, Golden Girls* and many other television shows.

If you have the time, the 'Backstage Studio Tour' is moderately entertaining. The 'walking' part of the tour is supposed to reveal some of the secrets of filming but it's rather dull. For cartoon enthusiasts, the Animation Tour offers a fascinating insight into the business of animation.

EPCOT (Experimental Prototype Community of Tomorrow)

This was the second part of Disney World, opened in 1982. It followed Walt Disney's dream for a place that would be 'a showcase to the world for the ingenuity and imagination of American free enterprise'. Unlike the Magic Kingdom, which simply entertains, EPCOT is supposed to entertain and inform.

For the most part, EPCOT is pretty dull stuff. A day will be more than adequate to see what you need to (you could manage it in half-a-day if you're pushed). EPCOT is divided into two parts: the World Showcase, which surrounds the lake, has 11 national pavilions designed to sum up the essence of each of the countries (Britain's main offering, for example, is a pub: is this really the best we can manage?). If it's not too hot, however, a walk around Showcase Lagoon is pleasant enough if only to see the replicas of the Eiffel Tower and Venice's Campanile.

There is better entertainment in Future World. These are the main attractions we liked best:

Captain EO ('Journey Into Imagination' pavilion): A mindboggling 3-D film directed by Francis Coppola and starring Michael Jackson with assorted furry animals on a 'musical adventure' in space. The 3-D effects are absolutely sensational (perhaps too sensational for those of a nervous disposition).

Cranium Command ('Wonders of Life'): A surprisingly hilarious account of life inside the head of a 12-year-old boy using Disney's most sophisticated array of special effects.

Body Wars ('Wonders of Life'): A high-speed ride through the human body. A similar experience similar to 'Star Tours', (see above), but less effectively realised.

In addition, children might enjoy 'The Making of Me' ('Wonders of Life'), a film on 'the mysterious, wonderful and often funny process of pregnancy and birth'. However, it goes so far round the houses to avoid the naming (or showing) of parts that children could end up more confused than when they went in.

The main attraction is in EPCOT's landmark, the 180ft-high 'geosphere'. This is 'Spaceship Earth', a ride 'through the dramatic history of human communications'. It is not worth queuing for.

Typhoon Lagoon

Disney's new water fun park has a good array of slides and raft rides. The best part is the terrifying wave machine which makes 8 feet waves every 90 seconds. An excellent day out, but put on plenty of sun tan lotion.

Admission Tickets

A one-day ticket which admits you to just one of the parks (either the Magic Kingdom, EPCOT or Disney-MGM) costs about £24 ($36.95); children aged three to nine £19.70 ($29.55). It makes more sense to buy either a four-day or five-day pass. A four-day pass costs about £88 ($132) or £69 ($103.50) for children; while a five-day pass costs about £119 ($179.60) or £95 ($142.60) for children. As well as admission to three main parks, the five-day pass also allows admission to Typhoon Lagoon, Pleasure Island, River Country and Discovery Island. You can buy your tickets with dollar traveller's cheques, American Express, Access or Visa cards.

Remember when leaving the parks, for same day re-admission to any of the three parks, get the back of your hand stamped with invisible ink that shows up under ultra-violet light (it shouldn't wash off in the swimming pool).

Tickets for Disney World in Orlando and Disneyland in California can be bought in the UK direct from Keith Prowse (0232 232425) or from Keith Prowse through your high street travel agency.

What to see after Disney

There are around 100 other attractions in the Orlando area, including star sights such as the Tupperware Museum (honestly). But after Disney, there are only three that I would recommend to fill up your remaining days:

Of the other major attractions: Universal Studios requires a full day. Depending on how fussed you are about killer whales etc, you could knock Sea World off in a morning or afternoon (the 'back-stage tour' is good because it allows you to see convalescing manatees etc). The Space Centre is excellent, especially for children: and because of the drive to and from the centre it will take up most of a day.

Any spare time can be filled with: Busch Gardens (two hours' drive away near Tampa) and Wet'n'Wild (water park in Orlando).

Throughout Orlando there are also dozens of 'factory outlets' which offer trainers, T-shirts, Levi's jeans etc at bargain rates. You can buy a pair of Levi's for around £13 (less than half the price charged in Britain).

Universal Studios (407-363 8000)

A one-day pass costs £23 ($35): children three to eleven, £19 ($28). A visit to Universal should take up no more than a full day. Orlando's newest theme park opened in 1990 and recently announced plans for a huge extension. Unlike the Universal Studios Tour in Hollywood, which takes visitors on a Glamor Tram ride through various special effects in the back-lot, Universal Studios in Orlando has a number of separate rides in the Disney style. Must-see rides include: Back to the Future, Earthquake and Kongfrontation – E.T.'s Adventure is also said to be good – it was out of service during my visit. For £16, you and your family can star in a special 10-minute episode of *Star Trek* sharing the screen with the original stars, with a video of your performance to take home.

Sea World of Florida (407-351 3600)

A one-day pass costs £23 ($35); children three to nine, £20 ($30). Claimed to be the world's most popular marine zoological park which offers a mixture of information and entertainment (the balance is on the entertainment). Performing killer whales, dolphins, sea lions etc; plus shark and penguin exhibits. Children love it.

Spaceport USA (407-452 0300)

A tour around the Kennedy Space Center provides a unique insight into the American space programme: bus tour £5 ($7.50): children three to twelve £3.35 ($5).

The other attraction within a short drive of Orlando, worth visiting if you have the time, is Busch Gardens (813-987 5000) in Tampa, with a good mix of roller coaster rides and African wildlife. A one-day pass for all ages costs £23 ($35).

Word of warning
With the spate of attacks against tourists over the last couple of years, this deserves some consideration. You need to be vigilant but not necessarily paranoid – be on the look-out for dangerous situations. If someone demands money and threatens you with a gun or knife, hand it over without delay. Always leave valuables in a safe at the hotel or in a secure place in your self-catering property.

Books
The best practical guide to Disney World is *The Unofficial Guide to Walt Disney World and EPCOT* (Prentice Hall, $7.95), available in most bookshops in the Orlando area. The 'official' guide to Walt Disney World (NOW Travel Guides, £7.95) by Stephen Birnbaum offers a rather too uncritical guide to the Disney attractions but has plenty of useful information.

Local Information
Orlando Convention and Visitors Bureau, 7208 Sand Lake Road, Orlando, Florida (407-363 5800).

9

A WEEKEND IN NEW YORK

Flying a few thousand miles across the Atlantic to spend just a weekend in the Big Apple might seem like a ridiculous extravagance. In fact it can make very good sense. Firstly, it isn't so expensive (several operators offer deals for around £350 for a return flight and a couple of nights accommodation). Secondly, a couple of nights is probably about as much of New York as any reasonably sane person could take.

Not that New York is a dangerous place to be (much to everyone's surprise it is way down the FBI league table of muggings and murders). It is just that the City That Never Sleeps can leave you exhausted. Take a flight from London on Friday morning, take a Sunday night flight back and you will have two full days and two full nights at your disposal.

FRIDAY NIGHT

After you've checked into your hotel and tossed your luggage into your room, hit the streets to take a look at Broadway and the night-life. When it's 8pm in New York it will be one o'clock in the morning UK time and you will probably feel more like collapsing into bed than venturing out.

Fight the tiredness and try to stay awake. My experience is that if you go to bed at 9pm you will wake up at three o'clock in the morning feeling ready to go – but at that hour of the night all that you will be able to do is to watch I Love Lucy on late-night TV. (If you are with children, try and keep them awake: there's nothing worse than everybody tossing and turning sleepless in the early hours of the morning. Try and get the children to have a sleep on the flight over – which should leave them ready for a burst of evening activity.)

By night taxis are the best way to get around: all licensed taxis are yellow. You can hail them when their roof light is illuminated – only licensed taxis can pick up people who hail them in the street (it goes without saying that you should not accept a ride from anybody else). All licensed taxis have a meter (many of which now issue printed receipts). Rates are reasonable: but remember to add a tip of 15 per cent (or you will be roundly abused). (It's worth asking at your hotel what fare you should expect to pay for your journey to avoid being ripped off.) Also bear in mind that unlike in London where taxi drivers have to undertake an extensive study of the city's streets to gain 'the Knowledge', in New York taxi driving is frequently a job taken up newly-arrived immigrants. Have a map with you when you take a taxi as you may well have to guide the driver to your destination!

So before heading to bed set yourself a couple of targets on your first night. The observatory at the Empire State Building is open every day from 9.30am to midnight (last admission 11.30pm). What better introduction to New York than to gaze down at it from a dizzying height of 1,250 feet.

For a closer look at real New York life head south and west a few blocks from the Empire State Buidling to the Empire Diner at 210 Tenth Avenue. You will quickly learn that eating is an activity central to American life, but New York is not just the city that never sleeps: it's the city that never stops eating. The Empire Diner, open 24 hours a day, is an Art Deco marvel – all stainless steel and black and chrome fittings. If you still have some energy check out a music club: for jazz there's the Blue Note club at 131 W Third or the famous Birdland at 2745 Broadway.

If you have bopped the night away and still have some appetite for sightseeing, take a taxi across the Brooklyn Bridge and watch the sun rise over New York harbour.

Saturday

Set your alarm for an earlyish start. If you haven't already booked tickets for a Broadway show from Britain, now is a good time for making plans. TKTS booths sell discounted tickets for plays and musicals on the day of performance (discounts vary between 25 and 50 per cent). The TKTS booth on Broadway at W 47th Street is open on Saturday from 10am to 2pm to sell matinee tickets (evening tickets are available from 3pm to 8pm). The Ticketmaster agency (212-307 7171) in Bloomingdale's on Lexington Avenue at 59th street also sells discounted tickets on the day of performance. Other agencies to call include Hit-Tix (202-564 8038), Telecharge (212-239 6200) and Ticket Central (202-279 4200).

Broadway tickets are expensive (expect to pay up to £45 per ticket for a popular musical). If you can't get tickets for anything you really want to see, go and see a movie instead: going to the cinema in America is to partake in a fascinating ritual of popcorn and soft-drink consumption. It's a particular treat to see a top film months before it opens in Britain.

Once you have planned your evening entertainment, devote the morning to the shops. Shops normally open Monday to

Saturday from 10am to 6pm – though the big department stores will usually open late night on Fridays, and many are now also open on a Sunday. New York is also the city that never stops shopping. Take a look at one or two of the big department stores like Macy's at 151 W 34th Street (which on 10 floors and covering one entire city block unashamedly bills itself as the largest store in the world), Bloomingdale's at 1000 Third Avenue or Bergdorf Goodman at 754 Seventh Avenue.

In almost every part of Manhattan you will find shops where you will be happy to browse for hours. Favourite shopping places include the South Street Seaport, just south of the Brooklyn Bridge. This old harbour area has been restored with a lively mixture of museums, shops and restaurants. Other happy hunting grounds for shoppers include Greenwich and East Villages, SoHo, Herald Square, the Lower East Side and Columbus and Amsterdam Avenues.

Shops that children will particularly enjoy include F A O Schwarz at 767 Fifth Avenue, generally reckoned to be the biggest and best toy shop in the world (at Christmas time queues often form just to get in!). Also worth a look are the Enchanted Forest at 85 Mercer Street and for books Books of Wonder at 132 Seventh Avenue which runs story-telling sessions for children.

Finding somewhere to have lunch will not be a problem. Eating places that children will enjoy include the ubiquitous Hard Rock Cafe at 221 W 57th Street and Planet Hollywood at 140 W 57th Street: other favourites include Peppermint Park at 1225 First Avenue and the chain of Ottomanelli's Cafes well known for their (large) hamburgers and their pasta.

Another outing children will enjoy is the Intrepid Sea-Air-Space Museum at Pier 86, at W 46th Street. The Intrepid is a Second World War aircraft carrier whose control rooms and flight decks can be visited – and there are a wide range of vintage aircraft on view.

If you are planning an evening out, now would be a good time to return to your hotel for a brief rest. Wandering around Manhattan is surprisingly exhausting.

SUNDAY

When you have the time, the best way to see the whole of Manhattan is to sail around it on a Circle Line (212-563 3200) boat. Since the round-trip takes three hours (during which you are treated to a fascinating array of ancedotes and history), you will probably have to give it a miss this time. But you can take a boat ride: go to Battery Park and get the ferry to Liberty Island for the trip across to the Statue of Liberty (open 9.30am to 5pm daily). Whether you climb the 354 steps to the top depends on the queue (it can be a wait of an hour or more at peak times).

Also worth a visit, just across the water from Liberty Island, is Ellis Island which was where around 17m immigrants entered American from 1892 until 1954. The complex of buildings on the island were restored and re-opened in 1990 as the Museum of Immigration.

Still on a theme of immigration and multi-culturalism, why not choose somewhere in Little Italy or Chinatown for lunch. The two neighbourhoods sit side by side on the Lower East Side.

The rest of the day, until you have to head back to the airport for the flight home, is probably best devoted to museums (museum shops are also some of the best places to buy presents). In the Museum of Modern Art at 11 W 53rd Street, for example, you can see The Starry Night by Van Gogh, Les Demoiselles d'Avignon by Picasso or La Clowness by Toulouse-Lautrec as well as modern American works by painters like Wyeth or examples of modern industrial design.

The main collection of New York museums is to be found on the Upper East Side on a stretch known as Museum Mile. Here you will find the Solomon R Guggenheim Museum at 1071 Fifth Avenue which has one of the best collections of modern art, with works by Chagall, Modigliani, Picasso and Manet. (The museum itself is a modern work of art, designed by architect Frank Lloyd Wright.)

The Metropolitan Museum of Art at 1000 Fifth Avenue is said to have one of the most comprehensive collections of art in the Western world with pieces ranging from prehistoric times to the present day with works by Van Gogh, Cezanne, a Rembrandt self-portrait, as well as Egyptian, Greek and Roman art.

The Whitney Museum of American Art at 945 Madison Avenue has a changing display of works by leading modern American artists such as Andy Warhol, Roy Lichtenstein, Edward Hopper and Jasper Johns. The Frich Collection at 1 E 70th Street has paintings by Constable, Turner, Holbein, Vermeer, Gainsborough and Whistler.

From Museum Mile stroll across Central Park to the American Museum of Natural History. You can spend an entire day simply exploring Central Park, a great New York institution in its own right. There are old attractions like The Dairy, which now houses the Visitor Center, and newly created places like Strawberry Fields created in memory of John Lennon who was shot dead at the entrance to the nearby Dakota Building.

The American Museum of Natural History is the largest museum of its sort in the world. Exhibits include the Star of India, the world's largest blue star sapphire; a replica of a blue whale; and the world's most cotmplete barosaurus specimen.

INTO WOLFE COUNTRY

One of the best ways to travel through America is in the footsteps of a book, a film or even a record. The most widely praised novel about New York life in the past 10 years has been *Bonfire of the Vanities* by Tom Wolfe. Using the novel as a guide book provides an intriguing insight into life in the Big Apple:

'Heu-heu-heu-heu-ganaaah!!! The taxi's engine is turning over but refuses to start. Where *are* we? Lost. In the jungle. 'I got gas. It ain't the gas, man.'

The name on the New York cab driver's permit says Jean A Modesta; the photo on the dashboard shows a young, anxious Haitian with a pencil-thin moustache and watery eyes. The eyes are now flicking this way and that, scanning the sidewalks for danger.

Heu-heu-heu-heu-ganaaah!!! 'Oh man, I don't think it's going to start...' A thick Caribbean voice tinged with French, edged with panic. *Ah doan tink he's goan star.* He walks to the front of his yellow cab, throws up the hood and stares hopelessly into the huge engine. 'Oh, man...'

We had been heading for the Bronx: into the heart of the jungle. I wasn't surprised that Jean A Modesta wasn't sure of the way. Being a New York cab driver seems to require the very minimum of qualifications – not even the ability to speak English. I gave him my map and he kept it next to him on the front seat. 'You have i-d about Bronx?,' said Jean A Modesta: 'He's a bad place, man.'

We cruised up Central Park West, block after block of elegant apartment buildings, women walking skeletal dogs. But then without warning we were in Harlem. In the space of a couple of hundred yards, the scene changed from affluence to devastation. This was Berlin in 1945. Row upon row of gutted buildings, blackened by smoke. Piles of stinking rubbish, people wandering about apparently without purpose, hopeless faces. A general feeling of danger. Jean A Modesta slipped the lock on his door. *Oh, man.*

But even with the help of my map, the Harlem river turned out to be a bridge too far. We join a freeway but there are too many exit roads, the overhead signs demand quick decisions. Take a right, take a left. Is that the George Washington Bridge? We are heading for New Jersey. *Oh, man.* We are lost.

He takes an off-ramp. The road twists through still more urban dereliction: abandoned cars, grafitti spray-painted concrete, *is that a BODY?*, bricked up shop fronts. *Where are we?* The engine dies. *Heu-heu-heu-heu-ganaaah!!!'*

Whaddaya whaddaya? You don't know the story of *The Bonfire of the Vanities*? What can I tell ya? Written three years ago by the very famous wise-acreing writer Tom Wolfe – the guy wears white suits and big brimmed hats – he's the new Balzac. Tell me about it. And I didn't even know there was an old Balzac.

Here's the tale. Big shot Sherman McCoy, regular Master of the Universe, has a million-bucks-a-year Wall Street job and a 2.6 million bucks Upper East Side apartment on Park Avenue to go with it. It ain't enough for this big shot. He's got a beautiful wife Judy, who gets by being an interior designer, and a daughter Campbell. Still not enough. So he's got this doll, name of Maria.

So one night Sherman is driving the doll Maria back into Manhattan from Kennedy airport in his black $48,000 Mercedes sports automobile. This road into town is some highway – no M4 motorway, believe me – a man can lose his way, especially if his mind ain't on it. ('Shuhmun, who's Christuphuh Muhlowe?').

Miss the off-ramp to Manhattan, and you could find yourself in the South Bronx. ('Sherman, I'm beginning not to like this.') This is the jungle. This ain't nice polite Park Avenue. Sherman and Maria are pretty scared, desperate to find a way out of the Bronx. But just as they think they're escaping, a tyre blocks the way up the ramp towards the George Washington Bridge. Sherman gets out. Two young men – black – on the ramp. *Yo! You need some help?* After a little rough-housing, Sherman and the doll Maria manage to get away: but at a price. *Thok! A little tap...*'the skinny boy was no longer standing...'

So that's how it starts. You think I'm gonna tell you the whole damn tale? Get outta here! We're talking a lotta words; we're talking *Great Expectations*. Maybe *La Comedie Humaine*. Whaddaya whaddaya?

Slip a fat copy of *The Bonfire of the Vanities* in your coat pocket and you can set out to discover the city of the book. Unlike Balzac's Paris or Dickens' London, both of which have changed beyond recognition, Wolfe's Manhattan is there complete and sometimes terrifying, awaiting inspection.

Start at the beginning with the dedication page. 'Doffing his hat the author dedicates this book to COUNSELOR EDDIE HAYES who walked among the flames pointing at the lurid lights...' Counselor Hayes practises law out of a New York office at 22 E 33rd street, formerly the premises of Warhol's *Interview* magazine: Warhol lithographs of Mao Tse Tung still fill the walls.

Hayes was working as an assistant District Attorney in homicide in the Bronx when he first met Wolfe ('I love that man, he's just a wonderful guy,' says Hayes). Wolfe was fascinated by Hayes's tales of life and death in the Bronx. 'Tom was a WASP (White Anglo-Saxon Protestant) from Virginia – this whole thing was an educational experience for him,' says Hayes. It was

Hayes's wife Susie who told Wolfe about how she got lost in Brooklyn coming back from Kennedy airport – Counselor Hayes reckons this probably provided the original idea for the book. Ed Hayes himself appears as the tough, street-smart lawyer Tommy Killian who defends McCoy.

It's a curious feeling talking to Hayes, a bit like travelling back in time to Dickens' London and being able to meet the model for Mr Micawber. I tell Hayes, the man 'who walked among the flames', about my plan to go up to the South Bronx. Is it safe to ride the subway up there? 'You might be lucky. You got an expensive watch...?'

When I get back to my hotel opposite Madison Square Garden on Seventh Avenue, patrol cars crowd the intersection, an ambulance is racing away. A policeman is mopping up blood from the sidewalk with a towel. *A huge black puddle of blood!!!* The policeman shouts to a colleague: 'You ain't gonna need this towel back, are ya?' His friend laughs.

On the TV, that day's news is awful. A retired policeman is shot dead trying to stop a subway mugging. A gang of 10 teenagers in Halloween masks go on a rampage of violence through a shanty town of homeless people – they murder one man by slashing his throat. Before several of the attacks, the police report that they said to their victims 'Trick or treat'. 'They were getting their jollies attacking the homeless,' said an investigator: 'It's like in the Central Park jogger case: when the blood gets flowing, people go crazy.'

Trick or treat? I decide not to ride the subway to the South Bronx. A yellow cab will be safer. *Oh, man.*

Before the Bronx, however, I check out the Park Avenue residence of Sherman McCoy. On the cab ride, the driver tells me that so far this year 36 cab drivers have been murdered. 'Gypsy cab drivers most of them, yer know wad I mean, unlicensed cabs: they drive after one o'clock in the morning. Where some of those guys go yer wouldn't want your ex-wife's mother to go, yer know what I'm telling you? This city's a big toilet,' he said, warming to his theme as we submarined through a succession of giant pot-holes: 'In three or four years New York's going to be a Third World city – nobody will speak English here anymore.'

In Sherman McCoy's part of the world on the Upper East Side – which is also Tom Wolfe's part of the city incidentally – there is definitely no sign of the Third World.

The book gives Sherman McCoy's address as 816 Park Avenue. There is no 816: running up from East 74th Street are 800, 812 and 820. The doorman at 812 ('all visitors must be announced') eyes me suspiciously. I show him my copy of *The Bonfire of the Vanities*.

'Ah, it's 800 you want. Dat's where dey did de film,' he says in a New York Irish accent so thick you could drink Guinness out of it. Another genial Irish doorman guards the way at 800. 'Sure, dis is de place. For de film, dey changed de numbers on de canopies. All de canopies up de street dey changed.'

The apartment blocks around here emit powerful vibrations of wealth. The McCoys had a tenth-floor duplex. ``The apartments were built like mansions, with eleven-, twelve-, thirteen-foot ceilings, vast entry galleries, staircases, servants' wings, herringbone-parquet floors, interior walls a foot thick, exterior walls as thick as a fort's, and fireplaces, fireplaces, fireplaces, even though the buildings were all built with central heating. A mansion!...anyone who put one foot in the entry gallery of the McCoy duplex on the tenth floor knew he was in...*one of those fabled apartments that the world, le monde, died for!*'

The place to look out for the real-life model of Peter Fallow, the English journalist, is one block from Sherman McCoy's fictional Park Avenue address. Mortimer's restaurant – called Leicester's in the book and also featured in the movie – is at 1057 Lexington Avenue. Just as Wolfe portrays it in the book, Mortimer's really is a gathering place for free-loading ex-patriate British journalists. Wolfe and the British clique which hangs out at Mortimer's seem to hold each other in mutual loathing – so no-one was surprised that Wolfe took a literary pop at them.

In the book, Fallow works for a muck-raking tabloid called *City Light*. In the book 'Scalp Grandma, then rob her' is the bizarre front-page headline on one edition. The real-life model for *City Light* is undoubtedly the New York Post which succeeded in uncovering much more grotesque stories than the ones Wolfe invents for *City Light*. During a notorious period when the Post was owned by Rupert Murdoch – and it was staffed by the flower of British gutter journalism – the paper was famous for its bizarre headlines: 'Headless body found in topless bar' is probably the most famous.

The main theme of *Bonfire* is the lawlessness and chaos that perpetually threatens to engulf mid-town Manhattan. Residents of $2m apartments on the Upper East Side continually live with the fear that the desolation of Harlem is no more than a few blocks away.

The symbol of this struggle of order against chaos is the Bronx County Building where McCoy eventually stands trial: nine storeys high and covering three city blocks from 161st to 158th Street. 'This island fortress of the Power, of the white people... this Gibraltar in the poor sad Sargasso Sea of the Bronx.' But the people with the Power stay inside the County Building, never daring to venture out into the mean streets of the Bronx –

even for lunch.

In Manhattan, it is a similar fear which keeps those with the money off the streets. From high rise apartments, they travel to their destination by limo. Those above a certain level of affluence would never dream of taking the subway. As Sherman McCoy says: 'If you could go breezing down the FDR Drive in a taxi, then why file into the trenches of the urban wars.'

To see what life is like in the front-line of the urban wars, I decided I had to travel up to the Bronx County Building. But Jean A Modesta and I never made it. *Oh, man.* I left Jean A Modesta at his taxi. 'You be careful, man. This is a dangerous place,' he said. I paid him the fare on the meter. I walked away and left him standing there waiting for help.

Where the hell was this? Me in my Marks & Spencer Harris Tweed jacket trying to look natural. *Yo! You need some help?* But there was deliverance: a subway station. Is it safe to ride the subway? *You might be lucky. You got an expensive watch...?*

This wasn't the Northern Line out of Belsize Park, but life on the platform seemed normal. I pay $1.15 for a token and wait for a train. We clatter back down town without incident.

I get back to my hotel room. There is a phone call. How did I get on in the South Bronx? *Whaddaya whaddaya!* Did I make it OK? 'It's a long Dickensian story,' I say. I'll write it down. Out of the jungle, and back amongst the literary sharp-shooters. It could be a cigarette ad for intellectuals: Come into Balzac country.

10

DIRECTORY OF US SPECIALIST OPERATORS

For each operator we show whether it is a member of ABTA (Association of British Travel Agents), has an Air Tour Organizer's Licence (ATOL), or whether it belongs to the Association of Independent Tour Operators (AITO): all of which guarantee that a company is bonded. Under new legislation all companies offering package travel should offer such protection but the law is patchily enforced – it would be wise to check with any operator before booking. For all purchases over £100 made with a credit card (Access or Visa), you are protected under the Consumer Credit Act. If the operator goes bust you can recover your money from the credit card company.

As well as a brief description of each company, the listing shows under which other sections of this book you can find more information about the holidays it offers.

Airtours
Holcombe Road, Helmshore,
Rossendale BB4 4NB
Admin: 0706 240033
Res: 0706 260000
Fax: 0706 212144
ABTA: 47064
ATOL: 1179
Credit cards: VISA ACCESS
'Airtours is the UK's third largest tour operator – taking over one million holiday-makers abroad every year. The company, which was set up in 1978, offers a choice of hotel and apartment holidays in destinations all over the world. Airtours offers thousands of free and reduced price child places for children up to the age of 19 years.'

America Ad Lib
Cranbrook House,
40 High Street, Edenbridge,
Kent TN8 5AJ
Admin: 0732 867307
Res: 0732 867300
Fax: 0732 867377
ABTA: 3978
Credit cards: VISA ACCESS
'The combined experience behind America Ad Lib totals over 50 years in travel and tourism.' The company offers independent fly/drive holidays, cruises, single- and multi-centre itineraries to destinations all over America.
Hotel holidays: all over USA
Self-catering holidays: Florida
Special interest holidays: fly/drive

American Adventures
45 High Street, Tunbridge
Wells, Kent TN1 1XL
Admin: 0892 511894
Res: 0892 511894
Fax: 0892 511896
ABTA: 2642
Camping adventure tours of North America. 'On an American Adventures holiday you'll share experiences in a small group of 13 (at the most) like minded fellow adventurers. In our unmarked "go anywhere" Maxiwagons you'll see and travel the real North America. An American tour leader accompanies each group to ensure that you make the most of your journey. He or she will help organise activities like river-rafting, hiking and horse-back riding as well as managing the food kitty, driving the vehicle, and conducting expert sightseeing tours.'
Special interest holidays: adventure holidays

American Airlines
Somerville House,
Steve Biko Way, Hounslow,
Middlesex TW3 3EE
Admin: 081-572 7878
Res: 081-572 7878
Fax: 081-577 1515
ABTA: 5615
ATOL: 2706
Credit cards: VISA ACCESS
Tour operating subsidiary of one of the longest-established US airlines. Fly/drive packages linked to its transatlantic services from the UK.
Special interest holidays: fly/drive

American Connections
7 York Way,
Lancaster Road, High
Wycombe, Bucks HP12 3PY
Admin: 0494 473273
Res: 0494 473173
Fax: 0494 473588
ABTA: 10619
ATOL: 2795
Credit cards: VISA ACCESS
American Connections, whose parent company – Abingdon Travel – has been trading since 1963, offers cruises, coach tours, rail tours, adventure trips, hotel accommodation, motor-homes and fly/drive holidays throughout America. The company operates a Help Desk which is manned by staff who are well travelled in North America – they can help with queries such as internal flights, stop-overs, airn passes and car hire. Scheduled flights are always used and holidays can be tailor-made to each client's requirements.
Hotel holidays: all over America
Special interest holidays: fly/drive, motor-homes, coach holidays, railway holidays, cruises

American Dream
1/7 Station Chambers, High
Street North, London E6 1JE
Admin: 081-552 1201
Res: 081-470 1181
Fax: 081-552 7726
ABTA: 26320
AITO
Credit cards: VISA AMEX
'The American Dream is a specialist American holiday

141

company. We offer a full range of inclusive holidays which we can customise to meet your particular needs.' The company has been in operation since 1979 and claims that staff have visited every destination featured in their brochure. It offers motor-homes, fly/drive, resort holidays, skiing holidays, cruising and city stays.

Hotel holidays: all over America

Special interest holidays: motor-homes, skiing, fly/drive, cruises, city breaks

American Independence

The Gables,
42b High Street, Great
Dunmow, Essex CM6 1AH
Admin: 0371 874848
Res: 0371 874848
Fax: 0371 874543
ABTA: 39674
Credit cards: VISA ACCESS
AMEX

American Independence, set up two years ago, is a specialist in tailor-made North American holidays. 'Whilst the objective was to be a year round tour operator, the primary strengths were in the USA skiing market. Last year we sent close to 2,000 skiers to America. The resorts have been chosen to provide a wide cross section of North American skiing – from the glitz of Aspen to the old world charm of New England. We provide holidays that are designed to your particular needs. You can fly when you want, from wherever is most convenient and stay as long as you wish. We offer only scheduled flights.' Included in the programme for the first time are catered chalets in Vail and Breckenridge and fly/drive add-ons to Florida can also be arranged. Launched this year is the Colorado and West brochure featuring fly/drives, motor-homes, pre-planned drive tours and coach tours in Arizona, New Mexico, Utah and Wyoming.

Special interest holidays: fly/drive, skiing, motorhomes, coach holidays, ranch holidays

American Round-Up

PO Box 126, Hemel
Hempstead, Herts HP3 0AZ
Admin: 0442 214621
Res: 0442 214621
Fax: 0442 214346
ATOL: 2921
AITO

'We are an independent company, specialising in ranch and river-rafting holidays in the USA. We have been trading since 1984 and carry approximately 500 people annually. Ranches are featured in Arizona, Colorado, Michigan, Montana, Texas and Utah. Riding tours are offered in Arizona, California, New Mexico and Wyoming. Special riding vacations are available at a mountain inn in Vermont, cattle drives in Wyoming and Montana and fast-paced horse drives in the High Sierra of California.'

Special interest holidays: ranch holidays, horse-riding, river running and rafting

Appleyard Tours
The Old Town Hall, Knutsford,
Cheshire WA16 6BY
Admin: 0565 653093
Res: 0565 755158
Fax: 0565 755373
ATOL: 2876
AITO
'We are a specialist tour oper-
ator, offering tailor-made pack-
ages to the United States. We
concentrate particularly on
touring holidays featuring
California, Florida, New
England, Arizona and the Mid
West. We offer fully escorted
tours featuring first class
hotels, comfortable coach trans-
port and interesting and
exciting itineraries, including
The Grand Canyon, Death
Valley, Hearst Castle and Cape
Cod. Our knowledge of New
England is extensive, here we
can offer whale watching, visits
to Shaker villages and historical
Boston tours.'
Special interest holidays: coach
holidays

Archers Tours
Linden House, 153/155 Masons
Hill, Bromley, Kent BR2 9HY
Admin: 081-466 4161
Res: 081-466 6745
ABTA: 1279
ATOL: 2862
Credit cards: VISA ACCESS
'Archers are part of the Cosmos
Group of travel companies,
market leaders in escorted
coach tours for over 30 years,
with offices in over 40 coun-
tries.'
Special interest holidays: coach
holidays

Backroads
4a Carlingford Road,
London NW3 1RX
Admin: 071-433 3413
Res: 071-433 3413
Credit cards: VISA ACCESS
This is an American company.
The address is 1516 Fifth Street,
Suite Q333, Berkeley, California
94710-1740. Backroads has been
organizing walking and bicy-
cling holidays since 1979.
Destinations in America
include California, Oregon,
Arizona, New Mexico, the
Rocky Mountains, Vermont,
Maine, Minnesota, Florida,
North Carolina, Virginia,
Mississippi and Louisiana.
Special interest holidays:
cycling holidays, walking and
trekking

Bon Voyage
18 Bellevue Road,
Southampton,
Hampshire SO1 2AY
Admin: 0703 330332
Res: 0703 330332
Fax: 0703 220248
ABTA: 17213
Credit cards: VISA ACCESS
Bon Voyage, a specialist in
North American holidays, has
been in operation for 12 years.
'Bon Voyage will arrange a
simple flight or fly/drive, an
escorted tour, a Caribbean
cruise, city stays, stopovers or
multi-centre itineraries. We
relish the challenge of special
interest holidays for golfers,
balloonists, mountain bikers or
American football freaks. We
are the first UK company to
have a computerised map

143

system that can plan clients' routes in detail, for instance a journey from Miami Airport to Miami Beach and then on to Orlando by car is printed out in great detail with road names, directions and mileage. In view of all the publicity about tourists getting lost we think this is one of the most desirable features we can provide.'

Hotel holidays: Florida, New England, Virginia, California, Hawaii

Self-catering holidays: Florida

Special interest holidays: city breaks, cruises

British Airways Holidays
Speedbird House, Heathrow
Airport, Hounslow, Middlesex
TW6 2JA
Admin: 0293 518022
Res: 0293 617000
Fax: 0293 552319
ABTA: 75416
ATOL: 2001
Credit cards: VISA ACCESS
AMEX DINERS
British Airways Holidays is a subsidiary of the airline. Its American programme includes self-drive tours, fly/drives, coach holidays, single- and multi-centre stays and cruises. Florida forms a large part of its operation.

Hotel holidays: Florida

Self-catering holidays: Florida

Special interest holidays: fly/drive, city breaks, ranch holidays, coach holidays, cruises

C&B Holidays
3 Peterhouse Parade, Grattons
Drive, Pound Hill, Crawley

RH10 3BA
Admin: 0293 886006
Res: 0293 886006
Fax: 0293 883025
ABTA: 7956
Credit cards: VISA ACCESS
C&B offers fly/drive holidays. 'We offer a variety of airlines operating from London's Heathrow and Gatwick airports and a choice of car rental companies. Our hotel voucher schemes give customers the choice of pre-purchasing accommodation in over 3,000 hotels throughout the USA. In addition we offer villas, apartments and selected hotels throughout the state of Florida.'

Special interest holidays:
Fly/drive

Caravan Abroad
56 Middle Street, Brockham,
Surrey RH3 7HW
Admin: 0737 842735
Res: 0737 842735
Fax: 0737 843242
ABTA: 3876
Credit cards: VISA ACCESS
'Launched in 1974, Caravan Abroad specialises in tenting and caravanning holidays worldwide.' The company offers passenger vans, tents with cars, tent trailers with cars, camper vans and motor-homes.

Special interest holidays:
motor-homes

Classic Tours
148 Curtain Road,
London EC2A 3AR
Admin: 071-613 4441
Res: 071-613 4441

Fax: 071-613 4024
ABTA: 47685
ATOL: 481
Credit cards: VISA ACCESS
'We have been organising trips to America for several years and due to their popularity we have expanded our programme to include more destinations. We are now the sole representatives in the UK for the tour operators, Mayflower Tours. As well as offering escorted tours, Clipper and Mississippi cruises, we specialise in tailor-made holidays for individuals, families and groups. Many of our holidays are arranged to tie in with themes such as jazz, country music and blues; civil war trails; antebellum mansions' and golf and sport packages.'
Special interest holidays: coach holidays, golfing holidays, steamboats, cruises

Club Med
106-110 Brompton Road,
London SW3 1JJ
Admin: 071-225 1066
Res: 071-581 1161
Fax: 071-581 4769
ABTA: 19685
ATOL: 1020
Credit cards: VISA ACCESS AMEX
'Club Med UK is part of Club Med SA which has been trading for 43 years. Club Med UK carries 25,000 people annually to 110 villages worldwide.' In America Club Med operates a skiing holiday at its village in Copper Mountain in the Rockies and has a village in Port St Lucie in Florida.
Special interest holidays: club holidays, skiing

Contiki Travel
Wells House, 15 Elmfield Road,
Bromley, Kent BR1 1LS
Admin: 081-290 6777
Res: 081-290 6422
Fax: 081-290 6569
ABTA: 20305
Credit cards: VISA ACCESS
Tours by coach for 18 to 35 year olds.
Special interest holidays: adventure holidays

Cosmos Coach Tours
Tourama House, 17 Homesdale Road, Bromley, Kent BR2 9LX
Admin: 081-464 3444
Res: 081-464 3477
Fax: 081-466 6640
ABTA: 24043
ATOL: 1082
Credit cards: VISA ACCESS
'Cosmos is part of a major international travel group that's the largest European coach tour operator worldwide. In over 30 years of operation we have carried around five million holidaymakers.' The company offers over 20 escorted coach tours throughout the USA.
Special interest holidays: coach holidays

Crystal Holidays
Crystal House, Arlington Road,
Surbiton KT6 6BW
Admin: 081-390 8737
Res: 081-399 5144
Fax: 081-390 6378
ABTA: 23816

ATOL: 1664
Credit cards: VISA ACCESS
Crystal Holidays was established in 1980 as a specialist ski operator. In North America, the company now offers East and West Coast skiing, as well as the Rockies, where it has operated for the last four years. It also features a lakes and mountains programme to Breckenridge and Vail in Colorado.
Hotel holidays: Colorado
Self-catering holidays: Colorado
Special interest holidays: skiing

Cunard
30a Pall Mall, London SW1Y 5LS
Admin: 071-491 3930
Res: 071-491 3930
Fax: 071-839 1837
ATOL: 264
Credit cards: VISA ACCESS
Bonded. Cunard has been operating since 1839. *Queen Elizabeth 2* is its flagship – 'the last of the world's glamorous superliners'. Among others, holidays featuring the *QE2* and Concorde, cruise holidays featuring New Orleans, Disney World and New York and inclusive American tours are offered.
Special interest holidays: cruises

DB Jazz Tours
37 Wood Street, Stratford-Upon-Avon CV37 6ES
Admin: 0789 267532
Res: 0789 267532
Fax: 0789 414644
ABTA: 14037
ATOL: 2288
Credit cards: VISA ACCESS

An independent company which has been in operation for over 16 years. It offers trips to jazz festivals around the world, including New Orleans.
Special interest holidays: music holidays

Donald Mackenzie
65-69 Bothwell Street, Glasgow G2 6TS
Admin: 041-221 5539
Res: 041-221 5539
Fax: 041-204 4381
ABTA: 4208
ATOL: 928
Credit cards: VISA ACCESS
Donald Mackenzie was established in 1925 as a small, family-owned shipping agency. It has grown over the years and now offers fly/drives, city breaks and escorted coach tours in the USA.
Special interest holidays: fly/drive, coach holidays, city breaks

Explore Worldwide
1 Frederick Street, Aldershot GU11 1LQ
Admin: 0252 333031
Res: 0252 319448
Fax: 0252 343170
ATOL: 2595
AITO
Credit cards: VISA ACCESS
'Small group exploratory holidays to more remote destinations. Formed in 1981, we are still an independent specialist operator with around 60 countries offered in our brochure. Our holidays include wildlife safaris, easy walks, major mountain treks, wilderness

experiences, raft and river journeys, sailtreks, seatreks and cultural tours. 10,000 people are carried annually to Europe, the Middle East, Africa, Asia, South and North America. Trips to North America include the national parks of California, the Grand Canyon and Alaska.'
Special interest holidays: adventure holidays

Falcon
Groundstar House, London Road, Crawley RH10 2TB
Admin: 061-745 4633
Res: 061-745 7000
Fax: 061-745 4533
ABTA: 68342
ATOL: 230
Credit cards: VISA ACCESS
'Falcon is part of the Owners Abroad Group plc, Britain's second largest tour operator.' It offers holidays to Florida, including hotel packages, fly/drives and cruises.
Hotel holidays: Florida
Self-catering holidays: Florida
Special interest holidays: fly/drive

Flightbookers
177/178 Tottenham Court Road, London W1P 0HN
Admin: 071-757 2800
Res: 071-757 2000
Fax: 071-757 2277
ABTA: 1470
ATOL: 2562
Credit cards: VISA ACCESS AMEX
'Flightbookers offers a range of products to the USA, including low cost flights, car hire, hotel and villa accommodation.

Open seven days a week, we are a fully licensed and bonded organisation with 24,000 clients in 1992.'
Hotel holidays: Florida, California
Self-catering holidays: Florida
Special interest holidays: city breaks

Florida Homes and Apartments
7 Astor House, Lichfield Road, Sutton Coldfield, West Midlands B74 2UQ
Admin: 021-323 2413
Res: 021-323 2413
Fax: 021-323 2417
'We offer a wide choice of homes and apartments throughout the Sunshine State. The accommodation ranges from one bedroom apartments and deluxe homes in Orlando to a five bedroom home in Key West.'
Self-catering holidays: Florida

Florida Vacations
23 Heritage Close,
St Albans, Herts AL3 4EB
Admin: 0727 841568
Res: 0727 841568
Fax: 0727 846326
ABTA: 2655
ATOL: 2976
AITO
Credit cards: VISA ACCESS
'As a specialist tour operator we offer a wide choice of areas and properties. Our selection features unique, privately owned villas and apartments, many of which you will not find anywhere else. Florida is the only destination we offer

147

and our service gives you flexible itineraries in one, two or more centres. All our properties have the following features: air conditioning, linens and towels, laundry facilities, fully equipped kitchen including dishwasher, colour television and private telephone. Our flydrive programme is arranged on scheduled services. Departures are daily from every major UK airport into every Florida airport.'

Self-catering holidays: Florida
Special interest holidays: fly/drive

Frontiers Travel
138 Devonshire Road,
London W4 2AW
Admin: 081-994 6958
Res: 081-742 1488
Fax: 081-742 1455
ABTA: 1644
ATOL: 2857
Credit cards: VISA ACCESS
AMEX DINERS
'Frontiers Travel is an independent tour operator established in 1988 specialising in holidays to the United States, Canada, Mexico and the Caribbean region. We offer to our clients (approximately 8,000 per annum), the individual, component parts of a regular holiday package allowing for flexibility and choice. Using only scheduled services, travel options include airpasses and flydrive holidays (car rental and motorhomes) plus a range of independent, preplanned itineraries. As well as 'Citibreak' destinations we

feature more than 60 centres nationwide and our clients can choose from almost 4,000 hotels, inns and lodges using 10 major hotel groups across North America. A separate Florida villa and apartment programme features a range of properties in Orlando and on the Gulf Coast. We are also able to offer 'add-on' travel packages to the Cayman Islands from points in the USA.'

Hotel holidays: all over America
Special interest holidays: motor-homes, fly/drive, city breaks

Funway Holidays
1 Elmfield Park,
Bromley, Kent BR1 1LU
Admin: 081-466 0333
Res: 081-466 0222
Fax: 081-313 3547
ABTA: 4703
ATOL: 2853
Credit cards: VISA ACCESS
This company offers fly/drive holidays, pre-planned fly-drive tours, motor-homes, escorted coach tours and hotel holidays.

Hotel holidays: Nevada, California, Florida
Special interest holidays: fly/drive, coach holidays, motor-homes, city breaks

Getaway
34 The Mall,
Bromley, Kent BR1 1TS
Admin: 081-313 1103
Res: 081-313 0550
Fax: 081-313 0620
ABTA: 96713
ATOL: 2819

Credit cards: VISA ACCESS
'Getaway has teamed up with British Airways to offer a programme to New England. The gateway to New England is Boston which British Airways serves daily non-stop from the UK. Bonuses from Getaway include a Rand McNally road map/travel planner with all fly-drive bookings, a Boston guide, a discount booklet and for children there is a ``Kids Love Boston'' guidebook.' The company offers preplanned fly/drives, escorted motor coach tours and weekend breaks to Boston.
Special interest holidays: fly/drive, coach holidays, city breaks

Golf USA

250 Imperial Drive, Rayners Lane, Harrow, Middx HA2 7HJ
Admin: 081-868 2970
Res: 081-868 2910
Fax: 081-868 2588
ABTA: 2918
Credit cards: VISA ACCESS
'Golf USA has been trading for two and a half years. We are a division of Ranch America. We carry around 400 passengers per year to Arizona, California, Colorado, South Carolina, Florida, Texas and Bermuda. Prices include flights, bed and breakfast accommodation, Hertz car hire and five rounds of golf, bookable one year in advance.'
Special interest holidays: golfing holidays

Goodwood Travel

Concorde House, Stour Street, Canterbury, Kent CT1 2NZ
Admin: 0227 763336
Res: 0227 763336
Fax: 0227 762417
ABTA: 33080
ATOL: 2249
Credit cards: VISA ACCESS
'We specialise exclusively in luxury tours with Concorde, the Orient-Express and *Queen Elizabeth 2*. The Flights of Fantasy programme is the world's largest and comprehensive selection of Concorde charter flights. These tours can be considered top of the range with, on many of them, exclusive events, gala banquets, magical moments and the finest hotels added to the supersonic thrill of Concorde.'
Special interest holidays: concorde holidays

Greaves Travel

33/34 Marylebone High Street, London W1M 3PF
Admin: 071-487 5687
Res: 071-487 5687
Fax: 071-486 0722
ABTA: 26496
Credit cards: VISA ACCESS
This company offers fly/drive holidays to 18 destinations across America. Flights are with British Airways.
Special interest holidays: fly/drive

Hawaiian Travel Centre

42 Upper Berkeley Street, London W1H 8AB
Admin: 071-706 4142
Res: 071-706 4142

Fax: 071-224 9184
ABTA: 33004
Credit cards: VISA ACCESS
'Our staff at the Hawaiian
Travel Centre have been
actively involved in tourism to
Hawaii for up to 25 years.' The
company offers a selection of
packaged and tailor-made holi-
days to Hawaii. Island hopping
and holidays which combine a
stay on the west coast of the
USA are also offered.
Hotel holidays: Hawaii

Hermis Travel
516-518 Fulham Road, Fulham
Broadway, London SW6 5NJ
Admin: 071-731 3979
Res: 071-731 3979
Fax: 071-736 1606
ABTA: 560
ATOL: 3039
Credit cards: VISA ACCESS
Hermis Travel operates holi-
days for Delta Air Lines. It
offers packages to Florida,
cruises, twin- and multi-centre
holidays, coach tours and
fly/drive. Delta fly from
Gatwick and Manchester to
Miami, Detroit, Cincinnati and
Atlanta.
Hotel holidays: all over
America
Self-catering holidays: Florida
Special interest holidays: fly/
drive, coach holidays, cruises

Infinity Tours
2 Molasses Row, Plantation
Wharf, London SW11 3TW
Admin: 071-924 3822
Res: 071-924 3822
Fax: 071-924 3171
Credit cards: VISA ACCESS

AMEX
'Infinity Tours is a newly established tour operator specialising in tailor-made travel for
groups and individuals. It is
part of a larger company called
Destination Marketing Ltd.'
Special interest holidays: tailor-
made

Inghams Travel
10-18 Putney Hill,
London SW15 6AX
Admin: 081-789 6555
Res: 081-780 2277
Fax: 081-785 2045
ABTA: 36750
ATOL: 25
Credit cards: VISA ACCESS
Inghams has been in operation
for almost 60 years and is part
of Swiss-owned Hotelplan
International, one of Europe's
largest holiday companies. It
offers skiing holidays in Europe
and North America, European
city breaks and holidays to
long-haul destinations such as
Mauritius, the Maldives and
the Seychelles.
Special interest holidays: skiing

Jetlife Holidays
33 Swanley Centre,
Swanley, Kent BR8 7TL
Admin: 0322 614701
Res: 0322 614801
Fax: 0322 615172
ABTA: 38031
ATOL: 2529
Credit cards: VISA ACCESS
AMEX DINERS
'We are a privately owned
company and have been
trading since May 1987. We
now arrange holidays for

35,000 clients annually. Our directors personally contract all elements of our holidays. Jetlife features all parts of the USA, the main areas being California and Florida plus the Hawaiian Islands, six Caribbean Islands and cruises. Our programme is based on scheduled flights from Gatwick, Heathrow, Manchester and Glasgow. We offer family holidays with up to two children, aged two to 11 years travelling at reduced prices.'
Hotel holidays: Florida, California
Self-catering holidays: Florida
Special interest holidays: fly/drive

Jetsave
Sussex House, London Road, East Grinstead, West Sussex RH19 1LD
Admin: 0342 328511
Res: 0342 312033
ABTA: 37556
ATOL: 1238
Credit cards: VISA ACCESS
'Jetsave has 20 year's experience in offering holidays to Florida and the rest of the USA. We have offices in Florida, Los Angeles, New York and San Francisco. Wherever you are in the USA you can pick up a telephone and dial 1-800 JETSAVE and you will be connected free of charge to our operations HQ.' Jetsave offer self-catering and hotel holidays as well as cruises, motor-homes, ranching and tours by coach, air, car and rail.
Hotel holidays: Florida,

Hawaii, all over America
Self-catering holidays: Florida, California
Special interest holidays: river boats, motorcycling, motorhomes, ranch holidays, cruises, coach holidays, railway holidays

Jetset Tours
Amadeus House, 52 George Street, Manchester M1 4HF
Admin: 061-953 0920
Res: 061-953 0920
Fax: 061-236 6693
ABTA: 37626
Credit cards: VISA ACCESS
Jetset has over 26 years of experience in world-wide travel. In the USA it offers scheduled flights, accommodation, fly/drives, sightseeing and coach tours and multi-centre holidays.
Hotel holidays: Hawaii, all over America
Special interest holidays: Fly/drive, city breaks, coach holidays, motor-homes

Keith Prowse
13 Cattle Street, St Helier, Jersey JE2 4WP
Admin: 0800 881882
Res: 0800 881882
Fax: 0534 69550
Credit cards: VISA ACCESS
Theatre and concert packages to New York.
Special interest holidays: theatre breaks

Key to America
15 Feltham Road, Ashford, Middlesex TW15 1DQ
Admin: 0784 248222

151

Res: 0784 248777
Fax: 0784 256658
ABTA: 38116
Credit cards: VISA ACCESS
Key to America specializes in holidays to the USA, offering inclusive packages and independent, tailor-made itineraries. 'Key to America's speciality is the freedom of choice. You may change the number of nights at each resort. You may reverse or change any of the holidays to include or omit any destination. And if you wish to do some business, or visit friends or relatives whilst away, either or both may be combined with any holiday.' The company provides a quotation based on your requirements and helps to plan your trip. All holidays are based on scheduled flights, and airports featured are: Heathrow, Gatwick, Stansted, Manchester and Glasgow.
Hotel holidays: Florida, California, Arizona, Hawaii
Self-catering holidays: Florida
Special interest holidays: city breaks, coach holidays, fly/drive, cruises

Kuoni Travel
Kuoni House, Dorking RH5 4AZ
Admin: 0306 742888
Res: 0306 742222
Fax: 0306 740719
ABTA: 35758
ATOL: 132
Credit cards: VISA ACCESS
The biggest selling specialist long-haul tour operator in the UK; part of the Kuoni travel group founded in Switzerland in 1906. It offers fly/drive tours, escorted coach tours, single- and multi-centre holidays.
Hotel holidays: Florida, Hawaii, Arizona
Special interest holidays: fly/drive, coach holidays

Longshot Golf Holidays
Meon House, College Street, Petersfield GU32 3JN
Admin: 0730 266561
Res: 0730 268621
Fax: 0730 268482
ABTA: 43788
ATOL: 16
AITO
Credit cards: VISA ACCESS AMEX DINERS
'Longshot Golf Holidays has been operating for 20 years.'
Special interest holidays: golfing holidays

Lotus Supertravel
Hobbs Court, Jacob Street, London SE1 2BT
Admin: 071-962 9933
Res: 071-962 9933
Fax: 071-962 9932
ABTA: 40489
ATOL: 1479
AITO
Credit cards: VISA ACCESS
Lotus Supertravel is part of the Lotus Leisure Group. It has been operating skiing holidays for around 30 years. In America it offers skiing holidays in Colorado but also offers resort holidays, golfing holidays and fly/drives in Florida.
Hotel holidays: Florida
Special interest holidays:

golfing holidays, fly/drive,
skiing

**Major and Mrs Holt's
Battlefield Tours**
The Golden Key Building, 15
Market Street, Sandwich CT13
9DA
Admin: 0304 612248
Res: 0304 612248
Fax: 0304 614930
ATOL: 2846
AITO
'Holt's Battlefield Tours is now
in its 17th year of operation. It
is currently part of the Green
Field Leisure Group and carries
more than 3,000 passengers
annually to all parts of the
world where there has been
conflict. Our tours to the US
feature a 10 day tour concen-
trating on Custer's Last Stand
and the Old West, as well as a
tour to the Cowboys of the
South West (Santa Fe Trail and
Grand Canyon). Our coverage
of the Civil War includes
Richmond/Gettysburg, the
Mississippi campaign and
Sherman's march to the sea
through Georgia. We also visit
the Confederate Air Force
Show in Texas. All our tours
are guided and expertly
researched.'
Special interest holidays: battlefield tours

Meon Travel
Meon House, College Street,
Petersfield GU32 3JN
Admin: 0730 266561
Res: 0730 268411
Fax: 0730 268482
ABTA: 43788

ATOL: 16
AITO
Credit cards: VISA ACCESS
AMEX
'Meon Travel has been trading
as a tour operator since 1968. It
has built up a reputation for
marketing quality private
homes – the majority of which
have swimming pools – in
Europe, the Caribbean, the
Canary Islands and Florida. We
carry around 500 people annually to Orlando, the Gulf coast
and Sarasota.'
Self-catering holidays: Florida

N.A.R. (UK) Ltd
America House, 1 Bolton Road,
Windsor, Berkshire SL4 3JW
Admin: 0753 855031
Res: 0753 855031
Fax: 0753 8551379
ABTA: 88740
Credit cards: VISA ACCESS
'NAR has specialised in organ-
ising the independent trav-
eller's individual needs to the
USA and Canada for over 12
years.'
Hotel holidays: Florida, all over
America
Self-catering holidays: Florida
Special interest holidays: coach
holidays

New England Country Homes
Grove Farm Barns, Fakenham,
Norfolk NR21 9NB
Admin: 0328 856666
Res: 0328 856666
Fax: 0328 856324
ATOL: 2984
Credit cards: VISA ACCESS
'We are offering relaxing holi-
days based in real, traditional-

style New England houses – homes of comfort and independence, charm and easy living. Our package, we determined, must be a complete one. Thus the parcel includes flights, car hire, property rental, insurances and first night hotel stopover. We have eschewed cities and large towns: our emphasis is on coastal and countrified. The local environs are rustic, small-townish, villagey, yet none are remote or isolated.'
Hotel holidays: New England
Self-catering holidays: New England

New England Inns and Resorts
1 Farm Way, Northwood, Middlesex HA6 3EG
Admin: 0923 821469
Res: 0923 821469
'New England Inns and Resorts has been in business for five years, offering a specialist consultancy and booking service, geared to the individual. In addition to the six New England states we are now also covering much of the rest of America. We believe that the planning of a holiday should be a pleasure and a lot of time is spent just talking to people to discover exactly what they want from their trip. We then put together an itinerary to suit them, together with making bookings in hotels, country inns, small B&Bs, working farms or self-catering accommodation. What we put together is not a pre-paid package holiday. People pay for their accommodation only once they have stayed in it.'
Self-catering holidays: New England

North America Travel Service
Kennedy Building, 7 Butts Court, Leeds LS1 5JP
Admin: 0532 425555
Res: 0532 432525
Fax: 0532 440481
ABTA: 3797
Credit cards: VISA ACCESS AMEX
'For the past 20 years our single market place has been North America. 25,000 passengers per year take the holidays which they have planned through the planning centres of North America Travel Service. Our holidays are available in all 50 states and are created with the client's itinerary in mind rather than fixed packages.'
Hotel holidays: all over America
Self-catering holidays: Florida, California
Special interest holidays: ranch holidays, river running and rafting, skiing

North American Vacations
Acorn House, 172/174 Albert Road, Jarrow NE32 5JA
Admin: 091-483 6226
Res: 091-483 6226
Fax: 091-430 1448
ABTA: 77977
Credit cards: VISA ACCESS
North American Vacations has been established for nine years. It offers a selection of hotels, tours, cruises and activity holi-

days throughout the USA. Clients are given the chance to build their own holiday, choosing from a variety of combinations.

Hotel holidays: all over America

Self-catering holidays: Florida

Special interest holidays: railway holidays, motor-homes, golfing holidays, river running and rafting, music holidays

Northwest Airlines
PO Box 45, Bexhill-on-Sea,
East Sussex TN40 1PY
Admin: 0424 732777
Res: 0424 732777
Fax: 0424 223300
ABTA: 29278
Credit cards: VISA ACCESS
Northwest offers inclusive holidays, city and resort stays, coach tours, fly/drive tours and ranch holidays. 'Because Northwest is a major scheduled transatlantic airline you can start your holiday on a day of your choice, decide how long to stay in the USA and return on the day you want. And there are flights from both London and Glasgow. You can choose holiday destinations in Florida, California or New England and you have the choice of one hotel at one resort or a combination of resorts.'
Hotel holidays: Florida
Special interest holidays: coach holidays, ranch holidays, fly/drive, city breaks

Norwegian Cruise Line
Brook House,
229/243 Shepherd's Bush Road,
Hammersmith,
London W6 7NL
Admin: 071-408 0046
Res: 071-408 0046
Fax: 081-748 4542
Credit cards: VISA ACCESS
'NCL is a division of Kloster Cruise. KCL conducts one of the largest cruise ship operations in the world. Its Royal Cruise Line, Royal Viking Line and Norwegian Cruise Line divisions offer sailings aboard eleven vessels. During 1993, KCL vessels were scheduled to call at over 150 ports on six continents, from Beijing to Barbados, from Trondheim to Toronto.' The company offers two-week cruises, fly/drives combined with cruises and holidays which include stays in Florida plus seven days cruising.
Special interest holidays: Cruises

Osprey Holidays
Broughton Market,
Edinburgh E43 6NU
Admin: 031-557 1180
Res: 031-557 1555
Fax: 031-557 1676
ABTA: 46644
ATOL: 749
Credit cards: VISA ACCESS
'Osprey is an Edinburgh based city holiday operator which has been trading for over 20 years. It is independent and privately owned and is run on a day to day basis by the directors. Osprey carries 16,000 clients annually. The holidays are flexible and clients can stay from one night to 28 nights.'

Special interest holidays: city breaks

Owners Abroad
2nd Floor, Astral Towers,
Betts Way, Crawley RH10 2GX
Admin: 0293 588104
Res: 0293 554444
Fax: 0293 588109
ATOL: 2600
Credit cards: VISA ACCESS
'Tjaereborg, Martin Rooks and Sunfare Holidays are the main direct-sell brands of the Owners Abroad Group, the second largest tour operator in the UK with its own airline Air 2000. Over 350,000 passengers travel with us every year to the most popular destinations including the USA.'
Hotel holidays: Florida
Self-catering holidays: Florida

Page & Moy
136-140 London Road,
Leicester LE2 1EN
Admin: 0533 542000
Res: 0533 524433
Fax: 0533 549949
ABTA: 47026
Credit cards: VISA
Page & Moy is part of the Barclays Bank Group and has been in operation for over 30 years. New itineraries for this year include the Deep South, Florida, the Eastern States and New York. All air travel is by scheduled flight. A new feature of all long haul tours is an included taxi service, if you live within 100 miles of the nearest featured airport, at the beginning and the end of your holiday. If you live outside the 100 mile radius you are eligible for either free standard class rail travel or free airport car parking.
Hotel holidays: Hawaii, California
Special interest holidays: coach holidays, city breaks

Peltours
Sovereign House,
11/19 Ballards Lane,
Finchley, London N3 1UX
Admin: 081-346 9144
Res: 081-346 9144
Fax: 081-343 0579
ABTA: 47685
ATOL: 481
Credit cards: VISA ACCESS
Worldwide tailor-made holiday specialists. Peltours uses scheduled flights from London, Manchester and Glasgow and offers US hotel stays in Arizona, California, Florida, New York and Nevada. The company has been operating specialist travel programmes for over 70 years.
Hotel holidays: Florida, California
Special interest holidays: city breaks

Peregor Travel
146 High Street,
Ruislip, Middlesex HA4 8LJ
Admin: 0895 639900
Res: 0895 639900
Fax: 0895 621026
ABTA: 47859
Credit cards: VISA ACCESS
Tour operator offering fly/drives, coach tours, city breaks, self-catering apartments and hotel stays.

Hotel holidays: all over America

Self-catering holidays: Florida, Colorado

Special interest holidays: fly/drive, coach holidays, city breaks

Premier Holidays
Westbrook, Milton Road,
 Cambridge CB4 1YQ
Admin: 0223 65626
Res: 0223 355977
Fax: 0223 324373
ABTA: 50118
ATOL: 2713
Credit cards: VISA ACCESS AMEX
'Premier has been arranging holidays for over 50 years. Our Florida programme features a choice of hotels and apartments in Orlando and the Florida beach resorts. With Premier, children pay a one-off child price, irrespective of the holiday duration. Add-ons are also available – a stay in Jamaica, a cruise to the Bahamas or the Caribbean. Breaks to New York, Boston or New Orleans can also be added to Florida holidays. For the remainder of the States we offer fully escorted coach tours, pre-planned self-drive itineraries or air tours that combine city breaks with beach stays.'
Hotel holidays: all over America
Self-catering holidays: Florida

Princess Cruises
77 New Oxford Street,
London WC1A 1PP
Admin: 071-831 1234
Res: 071-831 1881
Fax: 071-240 2805
ATOL: 3053
Credit cards: AMEX DINERS
'Princess Cruises (founded in 1965) became part of P&O in 1974. Princess offers the opportunity to combine a cruise with a holiday in America. Caribbean cruise passengers can opt to take a pre-cruise Florida stay of up to a week in either Orlando or Miami. Car hire options are also available. California is featured in conjunction with Mexican Riviera cruises whilst further north clients can explore Alaska. East coast cruises sail to New England and are combinable with New York stays. All holiday fares include return flights, accommodation, meals and entertainment on board plus port taxes. Free regional UK flights and a free hotel overnight at a London airport prior to the international flight are also offered.'
Special interest holidays: cruises

Ramblers Holidays
PO Box 43,
Welwyn Garden City AL8 6PQ
Admin: 0707 331133
Res: 0707 331133
Fax: 0707 333276
ABTA: 50940
ATOL: 990
Credit cards: VISA ACCESS
'Established in 1946, Ramblers Holidays is managed by a committee of voluntary members who are partly elected and partly nominated by the

Ramblers' Association. All profits not required for running the business are covenanted annually to a trust from which the Ramblers' Association can draw funds to support its work in helping to preserve and maintain footpath access to the British countryside. It carried over 10,000 passengers in 1992 and features holidays in Washington State, New England, Virginia, Hawaii, Arizona, Colorado and Canyonlands. All tours are graded and led by a Ramblers leader who arranges the day to day programme but there is no obligation to join the leader's party. The holidays are based on flexibility, informality and absence of regimentation.'
Special interest holidays: walking and trekking

Ranch America
250 Imperial Drive, Rayners Lane, Harrow, Middx HA2 7HJ
Admin: 081-868 2970
Res: 081-868 2910
Fax: 081-868 2588
ABTA: 2918
Credit cards: VISA ACCESS
Ranch America has been trading since 1988. We carry approximately 800 people per year. We feature ranches in Texas, Arizona, Wyoming, Colorado, Montana and New Mexico. Experienced and novice riders are catered for. We are able to offer over 50 ranches, from working ranches to dude and guest ranches.'
Special interest holidays: ranch holidays, river running and rafting, horse-riding, adventure holidays

Royal Caribbean Cruise Line
Royal Caribbean House,
Addlestone Road,
Weybridge, Surrey
Admin: 0932 820230
Res: 0932 820230
Fax: 0932 820248
'Royal Caribbean is one of the largest cruise lines in the world. The company was founded in 1968 by three Norwegian shipping companies. Royal Caribbean's Head Office is in Oslo, Norway and the operational Headquarters are in Miami, Florida.'
Special interest holidays: cruises

Saga Holidays
The Saga Building, Middelburg Square, Folkestone CT20 1AZ
Admin: 0800 300 600
Res: 0800 300 500
Fax: 0303 220391
ABTA: 36888
ATOL: 308
Credit cards: VISA ACCESS
'Saga has for over 40 years provided worldwide holidays exclusively for over-60s travellers.'
Special interest holidays: senior citizen

Ski Enterprise
Groundstar House, London Road, Crawley, West Sussex RH10 2TB
Admin: 061-237 3333
Res: 061-831 7000
Fax: 061-237 9311
ABTA: 68342

ATOL: 230
Credit cards: VISA ACCESS
'Ski Enterprise is part of Owners Abroad, the second largest UK tour operator. Ski Enterprise has been trading for 13 years and we now carry 80000 clients annually.'
Special interest holidays: skiing

Solo's Holidays
41 Watford Way, Hendon, London NW4 3JH
Admin: 081-202 0855
Res: 081-202 0855
Fax: 081-202 4749
ATOL: 559
AITO
Credit cards: VISA ACCESS
'Solo's Holidays has been trading for over 10 years. We provide holidays only for single people. We have two age groups, 30-50 and 50-69. A tour leader accompanies each group, acting as a social host as well as an organiser. We make an effort to achieve a good social mix of people without in any way operating as a match-making outfit.'
Special interest holidays: singles

Something Special Travel
10 Bull Plain, Hertford, Herts SG14 1DT
Admin: 0992 552231
Res: 0992 586999
Fax: 0992 587057
ABTA: 99336
ATOL: 2138
AITO
Credit cards: VISA ACCESS AMEX
'Something Special offers high quality, good value, direct sell villa holidays to Florida. You can take single or multi-centre holidays and stay near Orlando or on the coast in Hudson, New Port Richey, Tarpon Springs, Clearwater, St Petersburg, Sarasota, Longboat Key, Siesta Key, St Armands Key, Lido Key, Sanibel and Captiva, Naples or Marco Island. You can choose from charter or schedule flying arrangements or just rent a villa. The directors make frequent visits to Florida and so continually increase the range and quality of the homes. We insist on selling direct and not through travel agents, ensuring that prices are kept keen and that the client can speak directly to someone who knows the homes.'
Self-catering holidays: Florida

Sovereign Golf
Astral Towers,
Betts Way, Crawley, West Sussex RH10 2GX
Admin: 0293 599911
Res: 0293 599911
Fax: 0293 588322
ABTA: 68342
ATOL: 230
Credit cards: VISA ACCESS
Sovereign has been trading for 22 years. Sovereign Golf is a division of Owners Abroad Holidays, the UK's second largest tour operator. The company provides 'holidays for the enthusiast and beginner alike.' Destinations include Carolina and Florida.
Special interest holidays: golfing holidays

Specialtours
81a Elizabeth Street,
London SW3 4RD
Admin: 071-730 2297
Res: 071-730 3138
Fax: 071-823 5035
ATOL: 715
'Specialtours has over 20 years' experience in arranging escorted cultural tours to Europe, the United States and the Middle East, with the emphasis on art and architecture or archaeology.'
Special interest holidays: art & architecture tours

Sunworld
29-31 Elmfield Road,
Bromley, Kent BR1 1LT
Admin: 0532 393020
Res: 0532 393020
ABTA: 36746
ATOL: 1368
Sunworld is a trading name of Iberotravel Ltd. It offers holidays in Orlando, two centre holidays and fly/drives in Florida.
Hotel holidays: Florida
Special interest holidays: fly/drive

The Delta Queen Steamboat Co.
Acorn Travel House,
172/174 Albert Road, Jarrow,
Tyne & Wear NE32 5JA
Admin: 091 483 6226
Res: 091 483 6226
This American company has been offering steamboating holidays on board the Delta Queen and the Mississippi Queen since 1890. They are the only two overnight paddle-wheel steamboats still in existence. 'In the 19th century, steamboatin' was the way to travel in style. We've added comfort and convenience and maintained the authenticity that gave river travel its distinctive character. You'll find stained glass, brass beds and other antiques in many of the suites and staterooms. All rooms are comfortably climate-controlled and offer such amenities as an outside view for river watching, a private bath and plush wall-to-wall carpeting.'
Special interest holidays: steamboats

Thomas Cook
PO Box 36, Thorpe Wood,
Peterborough PE3 6SB
Admin: 0733 332255
Res: 0733 68519
Fax: 0733 505784
ABTA: 1921
ATOL: 265
Credit cards: VISA ACCESS AMEX
Thomas Cook has been in business for over 150 years. The company offers escorted coach tours, motor-homes, self-drive tours, mini-breaks, cruises, ranch holidays, treks, hotel and villa holidays.
Self-catering holidays: Florida
Special interest holidays: coach holidays, motor-homes, ranch holidays, city breaks, fly/drive, cruises

Thomson Holidays
Greater London House,
Hampstead Road, London
NW1 7SD
Admin: 071-387 9321
Res: 021 632 6282
Fax: 071-387 8451
ABTA: 58213
ATOL: 152
Credit cards: VISA ACCESS
'Thomson Holidays, Britain's largest holiday company, is part of Thomson Travel, which also owns a chain of travel agencies, Britannia Airways and other holiday companies. Thomson arranges holidays for around three million people each year.'
Special interest holidays: city breaks, fly/drive, coach holidays, motor-homes, honeymoons and weddings

Time Off
Chester Close, Chester Street,
London SW1X 7BQ
Admin: 071-235 8070
Res: 071-235 8070
Fax: 071-259 6093
ABTA: 58374
ATOL: 2315
AITO
Credit cards: VISA ACCESS
'We pioneered the development of city breaks – when Time Off started Paris was the only one on offer. We offer our clients flexibility in choosing how to get there and where to stay. We give them helpful guides, maps and a feeling that they are travelling independently, even though Time Off has put it all together. We have been in business for 26 years.'

Special interest holidays: city breaks

Trailfinders Travel Centre
42-50 Earls Court Road,
London W8 6EJ
Admin: 071-937 5400
Res: 071-937 5400
Fax: 071-937 9294
ABTA: 69701
ATOL: 1458
Credit cards: VISA ACCESS AMEX DINERS
'In business since 1970, Trailfinders has grown to become one of the UK's leading independent flight specialists and experts in tailor-made itineraries to the Far East, Australasia, USA, Canada and around the world. In 1992, Trailfinders carried 225,000 passengers overseas, approximately one third of these travelled to the USA and Canada. Trailfinders adopt a rather different approach to tour operators when selling their holidays to the USA. Rather than offer an off-the-shelf package holiday, the customer is invited to tailor-make their own travel arrangements by selecting the airline most convenient to their routing but more importantly, in accordance with their price range. The client can then select their own choice of hotels, ranging from budget to deluxe, car and motor-home hire and tours.'
Special interest holidays: tailor-made

Transamerica
3a Gatwick Metro Centre,
Balcombe Road, Horley,
Surrey RH6 9GA
Admin: 0293 774099
Res: 0293 774441
Fax: 0293 774061
ABTA: 96041
ATOL: 2499
Credit cards: VISA ACCESS
This company offers a fly/
drive programme, self-catering
holidays, cruises, motor-homes
and beach holidays.
Hotel holidays: Hawaii, Florida
Special interest holidays: fly/
drive, motor-homes, cruises

Transolar Travel
Transolar House, Wallasey
Village, Wallasey, Merseyside
L45 3LR
Admin: 051-630 3737
Res: 051-630 3737
Fax: 051-639 3578
ABTA: 58923
Credit cards: VISA ACCESS
'Transolar has over 25 years
experience in arranging holi-
days. All flights are provided
on the scheduled services of
British Airways, Delta Air
Lines and Virgin Atlantic
Airlines.' The company offers
fly/drives, holidays in Orlando
and on the beaches of Florida,
cruises and coach tours of
Western USA.
Hotel holidays: Florida
Special interest holidays: coach
holidays, fly/drive

Travel 4
Hill House, Highgate Hill,
London N19 5NA
Admin: 071-281 7833

Res: 071-281 6564
Fax: 071-281 8105
ABTA: 7230
'Travel 4 is a division of Travel
2 Ltd, which has over 10 years
of experience in planning and
arranging personalised tailor-
made itineraries.' The company
is a specialist in business and
holiday travel to the USA,
South America and Canada. All
flights are with KLM.
Special interest holidays: fly/
drive, coach holidays

Travelcoast
26 Crown Road, St Margarets,
Twickenham TW1 3EE
Admin: 081-891 2222
Res: 081-891 2222
Fax: 081-892 9588
ABTA: 3734
Credit cards: VISA ACCESS
Travelcoast offer the Florida
Self-Catering Directory, a
collection of villas, apartments
and condominiums. They offer
accommodation only.
Self-catering holidays: Florida

Travelpack
Clarendon House, Clarendon
Road, Eccles, Manchester M30
9AA
Admin: 061 707 4404
Res: 061 707 4404
Fax: 061 707 4403
ABTA: 7644
Credit cards: VISA ACCESS
Travelpack – 'the East Mid-
lands' leading tour operator'
offers a Florida programme
which includes self-catering
and hotel holidays but also
caters for holidaymakers who
have a specific interest in golf

or tennis.
Hotel holidays: Florida
Self-catering holidays: Florida
Special interest holidays:
golfing holidays

Travelscene
11/15 St Ann's Road, Harrow,
Middlesex HA1 1AS
Admin: 081-427 4445
Res: 081-427 4445
Fax: 081-861 3674
ABTA: 5956
ATOL: 34
AITO
Credit cards: VISA ACCESS
Travelscene has specialised in
city breaks for 25 years.' The
company offers short stays in
New York and Boston.
Special interest holidays: city
breaks, fly/drive

Travelsphere
Compass House, Rockingham
Road, Market Harborough,
Leics LE16 7QD
Admin: 0858 410818
Res: 0858 410456
Fax: 0858 432202
ABTA: 59381
ATOL: 1091
'Travelsphere is one of the
largest coach tour operators to
the USA. For much of our
programme, we offer a choice
of departure airports and the
opportunity to join the tour
from a selection of local departure points throughout the
country at no extra charge. We
only use the scheduled services
of major international airlines
on all holidays.'
Special interest holidays: coach
holidays

TrekAmerica
Trek House, The Bullring,
Deddington, Banbury,
Oxon OX15 0TT
Admin: 0869 38777
Res: 0869 38777
Fax: 0869 38846
ABTA: 60054
Credit cards: VISA ACCESS
'For over 23 years, TrekAmerica
has operated adventure,
camping tours throughout
North America. Trips are
arranged year round and last
from seven days to nine weeks
throughout the USA, Canada,
Alaska and Mexico. Trek
America aims to get away from
the package holiday approach
and specialises in off the beaten
path adventures for 18 to 38
year olds. Small groups of
never more than 13 passengers
travel in customised, air-conditioned maxi-vans accompanied
by an experienced guide.
Passengers are from all over the
world and the average
TrekAmerica group will
contain over six nationalities.
Various levels of adventure are
available with over 40 different
itineraries to choose from.
Many tours are designed with
the first time visitor in mind,
blending cities, small towns
and National Parks. The more
adventurous treks tend to focus
on the wilderness and Indian
lands of North America.
Mountain biking, water-skiing,
hiking, white water rafting,
horseback riding, hot springs,
campfires, sunsets and sunrises
are just a few of the outdoor
pursuits available en route.'

Special interest holidays: adventure holidays

Ultimate Holidays
Ultimate House, Twyford
Business Centre, London Road,
Bishops Stortford CM23 3YT
Admin: 0279 657776
Res: 0279 755527
Fax: 0279 655603
ABTA: 7841
ATOL: 2676
Credit cards: VISA ACCESS
Specialist tour operator offering hotel stays, self-catering accommodation, fly/drives and two-centre holidays in Florida only.
Hotel holidays: Florida
Self-catering holidays: Florida
Special interest holidays: fly/drive

Unijet Travel
Sandrocks, Rocky Lane,
Haywards Heath,
West Sussex RH16 4RH
Admin: 0444 459191
Res: 0444 459191
Fax: 0444 417100
ABTA: 61324
ATOL: 1121
Credit cards: VISA ACCESS
'Unijet has arranged flights and holidays for over one million people since 1981.' The company offers fly/drive, self-catering apartments in Florida, cruises, coach tours and holidays in Hawaii.
Hotel holidays: Florida, California, Hawaii
Self-catering holidays: Florida
Special interest holidays: coach holidays, fly/drive

United Vacations
PO Box 377,
Bromley, Kent BR1 1LY
Admin: 081-466 7766
Res: 081-313 0999
Fax: 081-313 3547
ABTA: 2784
ATOL: 2957
Credit cards: VISA ACCESS
United Vacations is the holiday programme of United Airlines. 'Our parent company, United Airlines, flies to 33 countries across five continents and to almost every one of America's states.' The company offers city stays, multi-centre holidays, fly/drives and coach tours.
Hotel holidays: Hawaii
Special interest holidays: fly/drive, coach holidays, city breaks

Virgin Holidays
The Galleria, Station Road,
Crawley RH1 2EZ
Admin: 0293 562944
Res: 0293 617181
Fax: 0293 536957
ABTA: 83588
ATOL: 2358
Credit cards: VISA ACCESS AMEX
'Virgin Holidays started in 1985. We are part of the Virgin Group and carry approximately 154,000 people annually. Destinations include California, Phoenix, Arizona, Florida, New England, Nashville, Memphis, New Orleans and New York. We offer a selection of two centre and tailor-made holidays. Much of our business takes the form of repeat bookings – we have five and a half

thousand Frequent Virgin families. When you go on a Virgin holiday, you fly Virgin, go to a Virgin Holidays hotel and are looked after by a Virgin representative. Five brochures featuring the USA are offered including a ski programme and Upper Class holidays.'
Hotel holidays: California, New England
Self-catering holidays: Florida
Special interest holidays: city breaks, ranch holidays, adventure holidays, skiing

Wallace Arnold Tours
Gelderd Road, Leeds LS12 6DH
Admin: 0532 636456
Res: 0532 310739
Fax: 0532 310436
ABTA: 62242
ATOL: 316
'Wallace Arnold Tours was founded in 1928. It is part of the Barr & Wallace Arnold Trust plc and currently carries over 300,000 people a year across all its programmes. Our tours to the US include scheduled flights, the services of specialist operators and good quality hotels throughout the trip. Our US holidays offer child reductions of up to 50%. Clients can extend their holidays either before or after the tour to allow extra time to visit friends and relatives or relax on a beach before flying home.'
Special interest holidays: coach holidays

Other titles in this series by Frank Barrett:

Family France

Family Italy (available in March 1994)